The Courthouse
Architecture for the Public Good

nai010 publishers

Contents

It is not possible to pick up a building for show and tell, so an informative book can be an excellent medium to present the finer details of a building to the public. This way anyone, anywhere can become acquainted with it. This book functions as a kind of guided tour with detailed descriptions and explanations to accompany the floor plans, elevations and photographs. Such a book serves to 'christen' a new building, like when a ship is christened with a bottle of champagne and wished safe journeys. In the new building, the book resides as a birth certificate on the coffee table.

The Amsterdam Courthouse simply calls for a book. The need is born first and foremost of its place as a public building, a manifestation of the rule of law that is administered publicly. The building gives a face to the government and symbolizes one of the three powers of state. On its own, this is reason enough to produce a book on the edifice. An additional reason is to share its story with the many visitors who come to the building. Hundreds of users pass through its doors, whether

to come to work or attend to important affairs.
Although one courthouse may differ vastly from another in the openness of its physical structure, a courthouse will always reflect the ritual of jurisdiction. And this requires some explanation, some words to draw connections, and some images with captions. Judges and other magistrates are not permitted to interact with the public as they walk through the building towards the courtrooms, since that could lead to interference or influence. The architect is faced with the challenge of disentangling the logistics, and how this is achieved is worth understanding. The architects of this building, KAAN Architecten, have therefore compiled and produced this publication.

The first section of the book covers the physical manifestation of the building. Ruud Brouwers describes its structure in terms of how it embodies the democratic rule of law and deliberately expresses openness, which also gives it a correspondingly agreeable spatiality filled with daylight. The building is woven into the fabric of the city, just as daily life and the law are. Brouwers sees an elegant efficiency and generous functionalism in the design approach of the architects. Such praise is fully verified once you have visited the building yourself.

The guided tour in and around the building then turns a corner by looking at the societal dimension of architecture. The second section of the book takes you behind the scenes through four dialogues with those involved with the building: Rijksvastgoedbedrijf representatives, Courthouse spokespersons and Amsterdam's urban planners. This provides a lot of background information on the demands of a public building, architectural conceptualization and public-private partnerships (PPS).

The courthouse was realized on the basis of a DBFMO contract. Kees Kaan and Vincent Panhuysen, principle architects at KAAN Architecten, explain how the architect is the central figure in the collaboration. Their years of experience have taught them that the architectural concept as a whole is integral to the success of a building. In collaboration with other consortium parties, the architect unites the required programme with the conceptual design into a sustainable, functional entity. Theirs is an enlightened point of view.

The distinguished, inviting feel of the building may seem easy to achieve, but its well-balanced and calm composition were no easy task, as a tour through the computer-generated designs will reveal. The fourth section offers an illuminating overview using drawings of the facade, courtrooms, ramps and gardens, along with construction photos

Finally, art critic Hans den Hartog Jager considers the contemplative character of art in the context of the new courthouse. Here he finds that the art, through its ability to express connection, interaction and truth, has figuratively stripped Lady Justice of her blindfold. He surveys not only the art directly linked to this specific building, but also the Courthouse's art collection.

I. Generously Functional

A M

In a democratic constitutional state, the administration of justice is a public affair. KAAN Architecten has managed to derive its source of inspiration from this theoretical principle in designing the new Amsterdam Courthouse building. By far the biggest of the 11 courthouses in the Netherlands, this architectural achievement is an example of purposeful and stately design, and succeeds in being both inviting and high-security. It is truly a dignified public building.

While old-style courthouses with their columns and tympanums often communicate authority and defence, this new courthouse has an unambiguously open nature. The choices regarding the functionality, comfort and sustainability contribute to this. The whole building is a well-balanced expression of democratic law. Its openness and serene spatiality are its essence and, in addition, the building is generous in its functionality.

RUUD BROUWERS

The Administration of Justice: A Dignified Public Affair

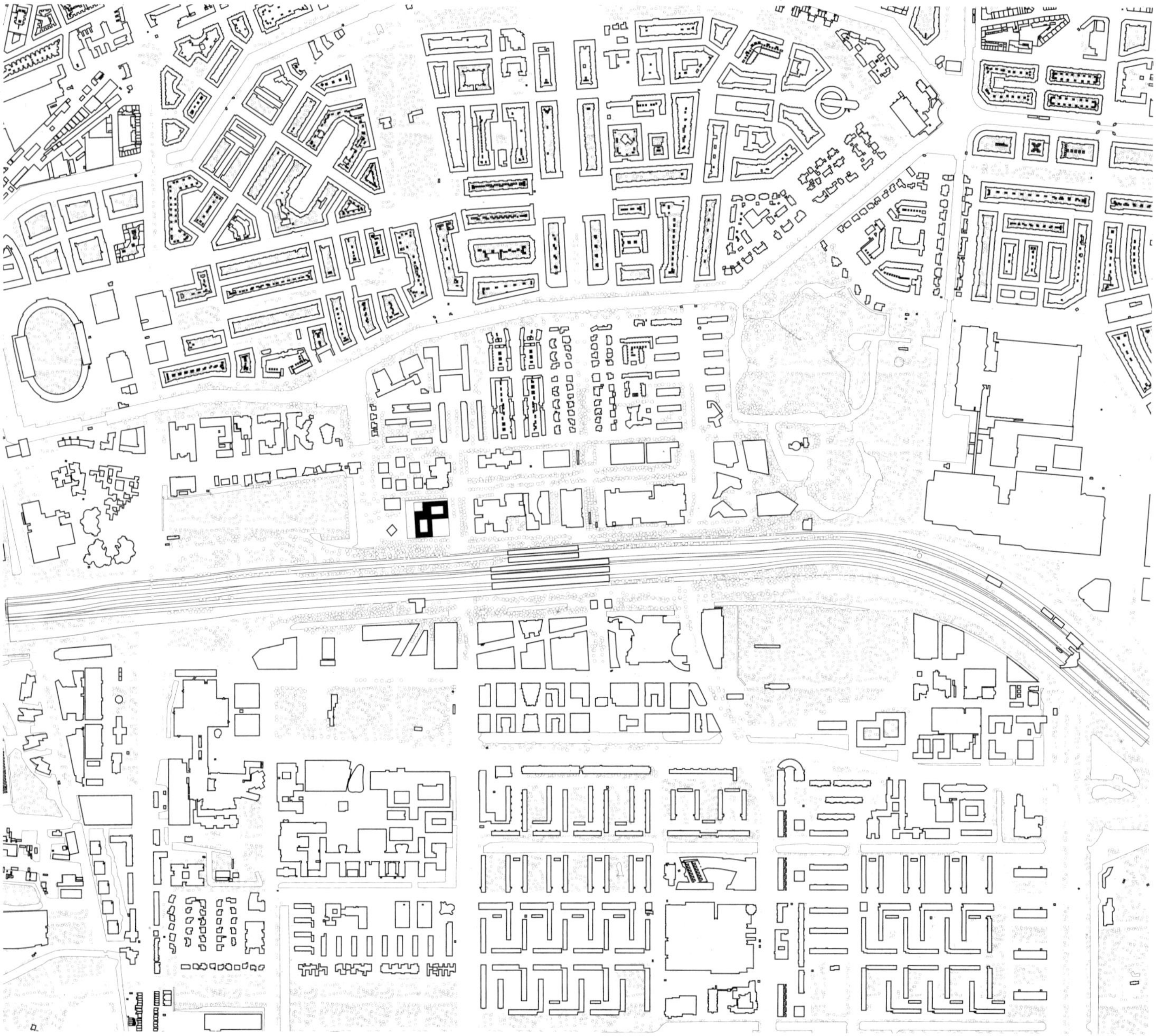

Positioned on the corner of Parnassusweg and Matthijs Vermeulenpad, the new Amsterdam Courthouse has replaced the old complex, which was a labyrinth of non-descript concrete structures. Only the old cantonal court designed by Ben Loerakker (1931-2021) is still standing, as this more refined, listed building waits for a new use. In the old demolished complex, people had to follow letters to find their way through the labyrinth. The meanderings were shortened when the decisive Courthouse President (1983-1993), Benjamin Jacques Asscher (1925-2008) commissioned a bridge between the two structures – the only attractive feature of the complex. Mr Asscher, incidentally, very much believed in the public nature of jurisdiction; the new courthouse would have pleased him.

The reserved yet robust architectural presence of the new courthouse dovetails nicely into the austere yet spacious plan of the surrounding post-war city: the South-Amstel-Canal plan by urbanist Cornelis van Eesteren (1897-1988) and the more expressive Amsterdam-Zuid/Stadium district plan by architect Hendrik Petrus Berlage (1856-1934). Van Eesteren's urban plan is a fine-grained grid with a hierarchy of perpendicular main roads, bicycle paths, footpaths and green lines, almost like a Scottish tartan. The new building, in all its stateliness, still acknowledges its neighbours. The open urban pattern with square building blocks is loosely pulled into the layout of the new courthouse. It also presents four full faces to the outside world – there are no backsides.

The building seems to emerge from the grid through its base, which rises 90 centimetres. While this rise is not even a metre high, it is a significant security element as it safeguards against ram-raiding and also provides easier road access to the basement (though there are also ramps). Designing the access into the building was also an opportunity to move the holding cells for detainees/defendants from the ground floor to the basement level. The holding area and the space needed for the transportation of detainees (separate entrances, screened-off exits) requires quite a lot of room. The ground floor has been reserved as much as possible for the entrance hall and the central hall, the latter being a culmination of spaciousness affording oversight to all users and visitors. These halls really function as an extension of the city. It is the ground floor also that has the largest courtrooms to accommodate the greatest number of visitors, such as the extra-large courtroom with more gallery space for those cases that attract the public.

INTEGRATING THE BUILDING INTO THE URBAN FABRIC

A public square with a reflecting pool on the south side, the main entrance to the courthouse, is where building and city meet. Here is the moment of transition, and hence the purest opportunity for integration. The square is in fact a quarter of the entire building site, it is paved in the same light grey stone as the building, and it has the same benches as inside. The lean and subtle canopy over the entrance stretches an equal distance into and out of the building.

As public space, the square of course makes a gesture to the city. A low-rising ramp minimizes any sense of obstruction between the surroundings and the square, which is actually slightly raised. One side of the square has been planted with decorative trees, providing a place to relax not only for staff and courthouse visitors, but everyone in the area at any time of day. Given his advocacy of the public nature of jurisdiction, naming the square after B.J. Asscher would not be misplaced.

The courthouse square finds parallels in Berlage's Amsterdam-Zuid, not only in its scale (at half a football pitch), but also in architectural richness: the restrained though meticulously designed courthouse facades, the pool and the large sculpture *Love or Generosity* by artist Nicole Eisenman. The architect and the art committee wanted a tall sculptural form as a transition between building and square. The gender-neutral figure in track trousers and gigantic hiking boots is bending forward with symbols in its hand that stand for wisdom, strength, patience, progress and courage. A small owl, an arrow and an acorn, which represent the resilience of society, seem to have just been picked up from the square. Perhaps the young giant is actually showing us the symbol while bending over to protect them in its hand. The informal nature might also encourage children to climb into the hand and hide behind the symbols.

The square is flanked on two sides by the 23-metre pilasters of the building, clad in the same light grey stone as the square. Between the pilasters, sheets of glazing rise high and offer views into and out of the building. The height is determined by the central hall with its cafeteria, courtrooms, and the adjacent rooms and foyers. The quality glazing means there are little to no reflections obstructing the views. The foyers guide users like visitors, lawyers and reporters around and towards the courtrooms.

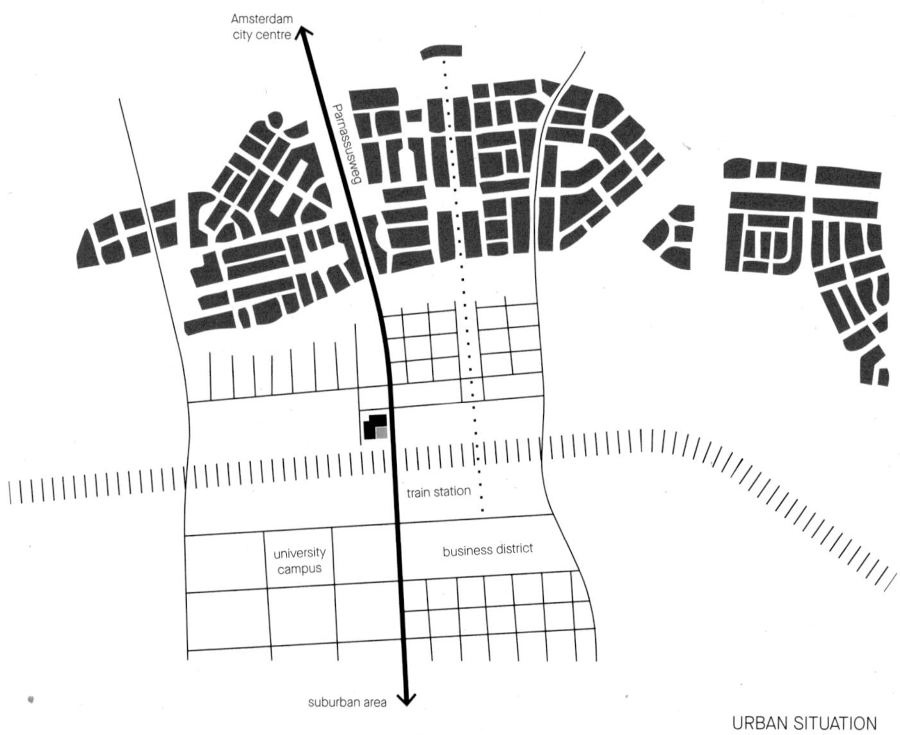

URBAN SITUATION

These spaces are part of city life, the administration of justice being part of daily life. Anyone visiting the courthouse for whatever reason can remain anonymous if they so choose by using the sheltered spaces furnished with leather-upholstered, high-backed benches turned away from outside eyes.

The Amsterdam Courthouse is 50 metres tall and is situated next to and opposite the buildings of Amsterdam's Vrije Universiteit and other buildings of the new Zuidas business district – 245 hectares of office buildings and residential flats serviced by train, tram, metro lines, a network of cycling paths and a wide ring road that will soon go underground. Train station Zuid is very close by and once all the construction work in the area is complete, it will become just as busy as Amsterdam's Centraal Station. The Zuidas district is still under development, but eventually an important linking street for slow traffic will run alongside the courthouse's square. The transport link to both Schiphol Airport and the city centre with its famous canals should ensure that the Zuidas area will become well-integrated with the city, and that Amsterdam will not just be a tourist city, but also well-known for its international service and trade industries.

The high-rise offices of the Zuidas need to be representative of the professionalism of their occupants and display a standing on par with international peers. This is testified to by the works of famous architects like Toyo Ito, Rafael Viñoly, SOM, Michael Graves and a few internationally recognized Dutch firms. It's almost a competition: Who will be crowned the king of the Zuidas? In the middle of this architectural rivalry stands the Amsterdam Courthouse, and it reigns supreme with its noble simplicity and composed friendliness. Its distinguished architectural form and its public accessibility have given the Zuidas an extra energy. Next to the residential high-rises, the courthouse has made the Zuidas, as a Central Business District (CBD), a more complete city.

BEYOND VAIN FRIVOLITIES

The design principles, detailing and functional precision inextricably anchor the building in its public purpose and place it in a realm free of frivolities. The voluminous central hall allows for both vitality and serenity, and this makes it immediately clear that it is an important public space and one that houses an important institution. The visual division of the exterior into three main levels, with a crown of windows for excellent city views, gives substance to the building, as do the facades' patterns and the rising stone pilasters that flank the square. Together with the facades' dark steel verticals and transparent glass, the structure emanates dignity – like a judge's robe or like sparkling eyes set off by mascara. The slender, inconspicuous profiles supporting the glazing are very much a contemporary aesthetic, though the balanced proportions are timeless.

The building's striking architecture is a result of integrating it with its environment, including the square, and fusing the separate elements of the programme in consideration of this. More specifically: it is a result of how the holding area for detainees (a complex of cells), courtrooms plus foyers, office spaces and the so-called transition zone have been given a proper place in relation to each other. The publicly accessible area takes up 23 metres of the building's elevation, from street level to the four floors with generous heights, and even double-heights for the courtrooms. The fifth-floor offices needed to be closed off and are logically housed in the upper levels with generous windows. This functional three-part stacking (street level – transition zone – offices) has been beautifully expressed in the facades, giving a face to the whole as well as organizing its shape.

A variety of judicial bodies have regular contact with the Courthouse, though with the exception of only a few, these are not housed in the building itself, based on the independence of the institution. Representatives of judicial authorities include judges, public prosecutors, police officers, and professionals from the Ministry of Justice, penitentiaries, probation and youth welfare. These people meet each other in the transition zone for consultations and deliberations. For reasons of confidentiality this always occurs away from the public eye. The Amsterdam Courthouse is a central meeting place for the whole country on account of its good connections and accommodations. Legal staff of the Courthouse also meet up in the transition zone to discuss and coordinate matters, and share expertise and experiences. In this regard, the area is a hub of knowledge and wisdom. The area has meeting rooms, most of which have views over the city, informal spaces for ad-hoc encounters, and a centre of expertise linked to the library.

Suitably located in the transition zone are the restaurant and enclosed terrace with outdoor work stations. The terrace is on the west side and is two storeys high with the facade pilasters continuing uninterrupted, though free of glazing. The supporting structure of verticals retains a firm presence and keeps the 'three-piece tailoring' of the building intact. The multitude of uses and activities in the transition zone requires a crystal-clear layout, for here one can research case law, eat a sandwich, share information or review rulings. Orientation is made easy by the high and wide 'street' that runs the full length from east to west and connects all the spaces in the transition zone.

JUDGES USE SEPARATE LIFTS

The tripartite stacking that gives the facades such clarity and expression is also a feature of multi-functionality. The ceremony of administering justice is strictly bound by rules, which is what allows it to be a public affair. Due process means that in order to avoid any opportunities for influencing judges, they must be able to walk to and from a courtroom without any kind of contact with detainees or visitors, among which are defendants, litigants and lawyers. The judges travel directly from their offices or transition zone by separate lifts down to the courtrooms, and enter the area by screened-off corridors behind the courtrooms and deliberation chambers. This is also the process for public prosecutors and court clerks, though from a different point of entry.

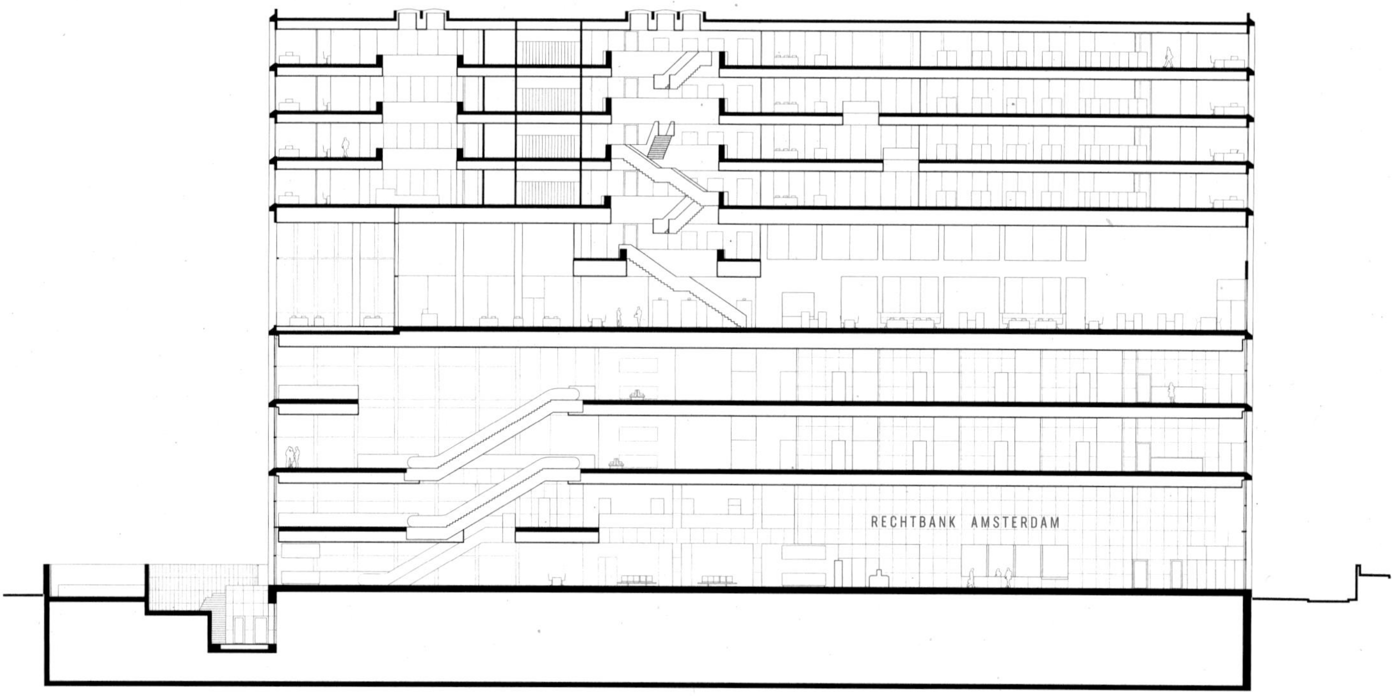

SECTION

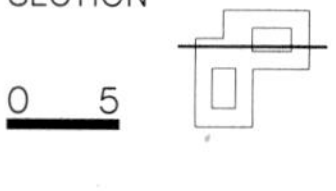

Detainees who are due in court are also brought up from the cells below by way of a separate route and separate lifts, under the watch of the Amsterdam Security, Surveillance & Transport (SS&T).

The building's footprint, 87.7 by 87.7 metres, already tells us that the courthouse is an enormous and complex organization. It employs 1,000 to 1,200 people, including 200 judges. Every day some 800 to 1,000 visitors pass through its doors. Around 140,000 verdicts are reached every year, which of course involves a lot of administrative work as well. The Amsterdam Courthouse is divided into three departments: Private law with teams for Trade, Insolvency and Administration, Preliminary Injunctions, Family and Youth Affairs, and lower court issues; Public law with teams for Administrative Law and Criminal Law; and a Staff department with support services and SS&T.

The operational base of these departments are the five office floors, additional rooms for concentrated study, and a network of nearly 13 metres of dossier carts. The Courthouse management board is also housed here. To encourage contact and discussions, there are many open and informal spots all around the office area, and floors that open up into spacious stairwells. The wide circles that accommodate the stairs are directly above each other, though the stairs themselves rise in different directions through the space, producing a spectacular composition reminiscent of Piranesi's prints – though without the sinister feel.

Internal traffic is serviced by lifts and stairs. The dossier carts come to around chest height, leaving enough space for oversight everywhere. 'Don't let your brain sit around,' is the advice of Erik Scherder, Professor of Neuropsychology, and this has been taken to heart. Rather than constantly sitting down to work, all worktops can be raised in order to stand at them. The mood is minimalist, though not in the sense of having been frugal. It is precision and attention to detail – details important to ambience and health, details serving comfort and functionality.

Daylight floods in thanks to the ample windows on all sides. Particular aspects of the building's envelope were modified in order to allow daylight to fully penetrate into the heart of the building. For example, the north-west corner (diagonally opposite the square) was opened up for daylight and to subdue the building with respect to its surroundings. The ideal way to fill such an opening is with gardens. The walled corner garden has greenery that shoots above the garden wall to imbue a sense of neighbourliness. Within the building the garden is in full view, though enclosed: a *hortus conclusus* with flowers, trees, shrubs and sculptures, open only for staff get-togethers. Cutting into the corner of the building produced a stunning extra dimension to the grid: light just streams into the sea of space that is the central hall. More light enters the building from top to bottom through the large skylights. Light funnels through the office floors to the public areas below. Lush, full-height vertical gardens stretch over the office courtyards and contribute a pleasant climate where you can also open windows.

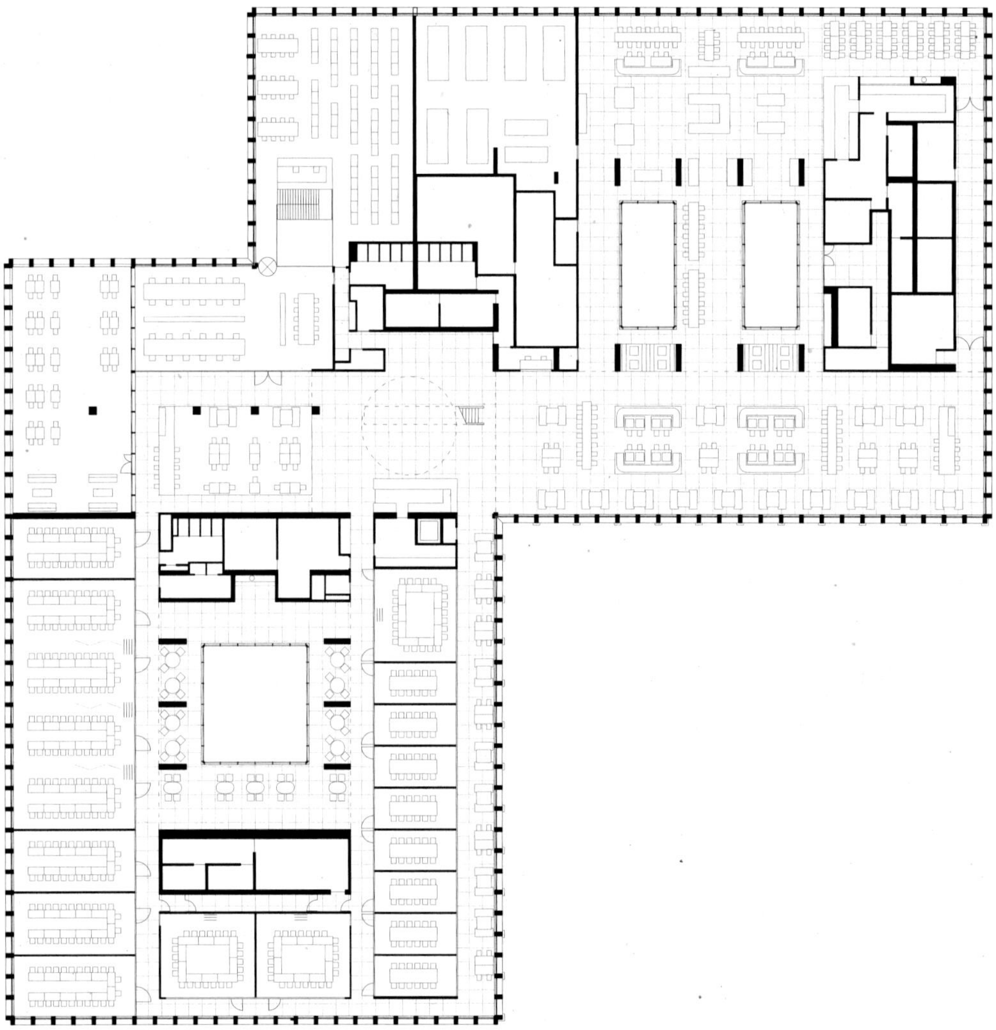

FLOOR PLAN +5

0 5 N

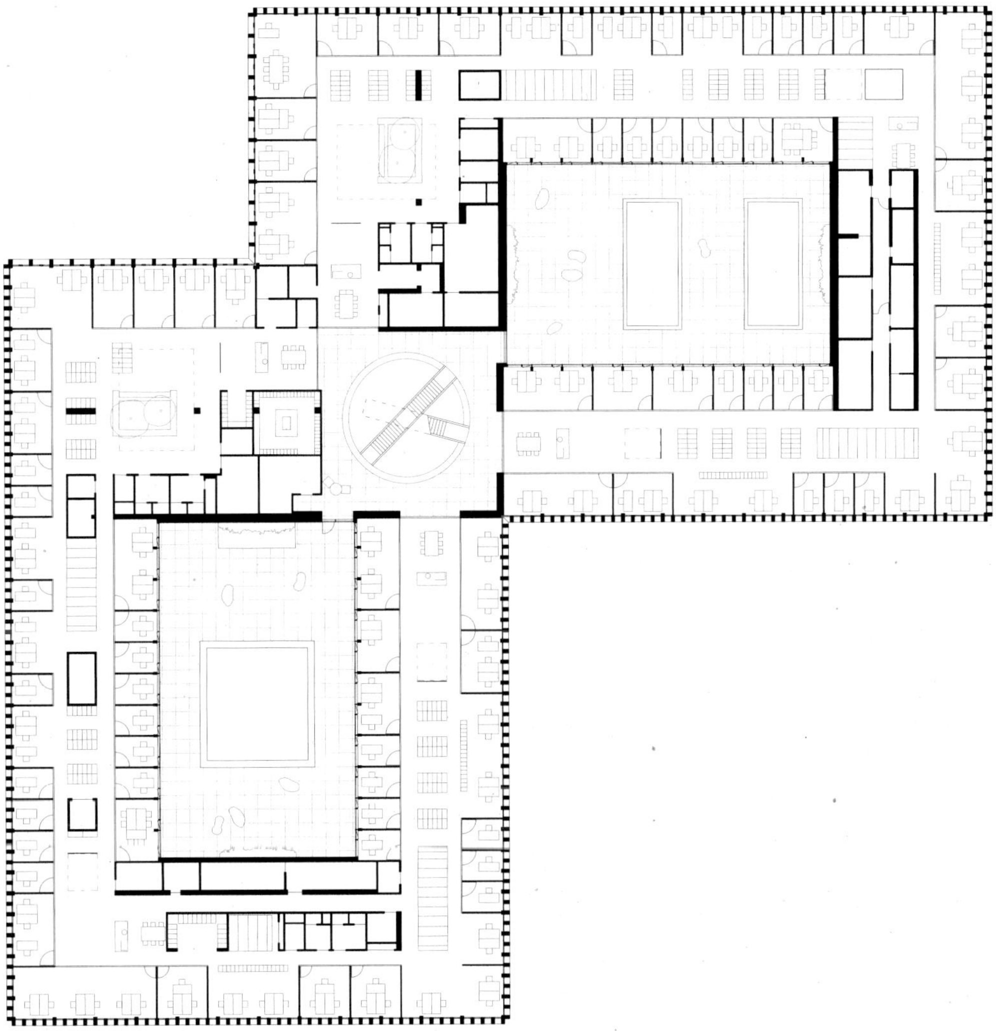

FLOOR PLAN +7

0 5 N

The central hall is the beating heart of the building. It is at the same level as the square out front, and after coming through the entrance hall and security checks, it provides an opportunity for orientation, also in terms of vertical directions. From this 23-metre-high space appear 'two buildings in the building' hosting the courtrooms, the interview rooms, the counsel chambers – all of which adds up to 50 rooms for public use. Everything is connected by the escalators that run alongside a wall of glass that encloses the inner garden. The escalator experience is like that in a museum. The central hall also displays a large portion of the Courthouse's impressive art collection.

The floors above the central hall are open, making the areas outside the courtrooms feel like walkways with views over the railing and sightlines through to other floors. All this spaciousness is made possible by the supporting structure: loadbearing facades and a minimum of internal columns deliver a building in which space flows freely, unobstructed by rows of columns. The entrance and central hall are clad in light grey stone, right up to the courtroom foyers and in continuation of the outside square. Consortium NACH (New Amsterdam Court House) is obliged, on the basis of the 30-year Public-Private Partnership contract with the government, to maintain the property and so chose durable materials to reduce costs.

SURVEILLANCE CAMERAS UNNECESSARY

The foyers to the courtrooms are found on the 'window sides' of the building, or in other words, the space between the glazed exterior wall and the stone-clad and plastered walls enclosing the courtrooms. Through these spacious corridors and with views over the city walk lawyers in their billowing robes, their clients and the public. There is often a great deal of activity here. Every floor has strategically positioned desks to which visitors report and from which the courtroom doors are monitored, so surveillance cameras are unnecessary. The desks have a friendly organic shape with canopy and a letter to indicate its address.

Various amenities connect the central hall with the courtrooms, which have black and white external walls, like robe and collar. On the one side run the escalators along the enclosed garden and on the other is the first-floor cafeteria. In addition to the general reception desk for visitors and the press, the Central Information Desk is an important point in the whole as it is connects with the centre of expertise and library – one of the best equipped legal libraries in the country. The press room offers something new: the ability to follow proceedings remotely.

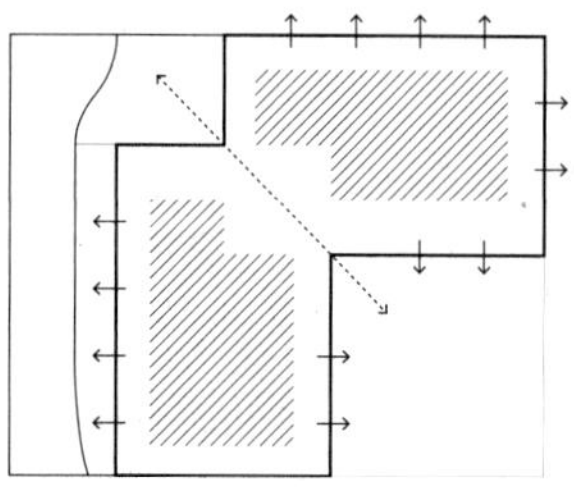

VISIBILITY FROM ALL SIDES

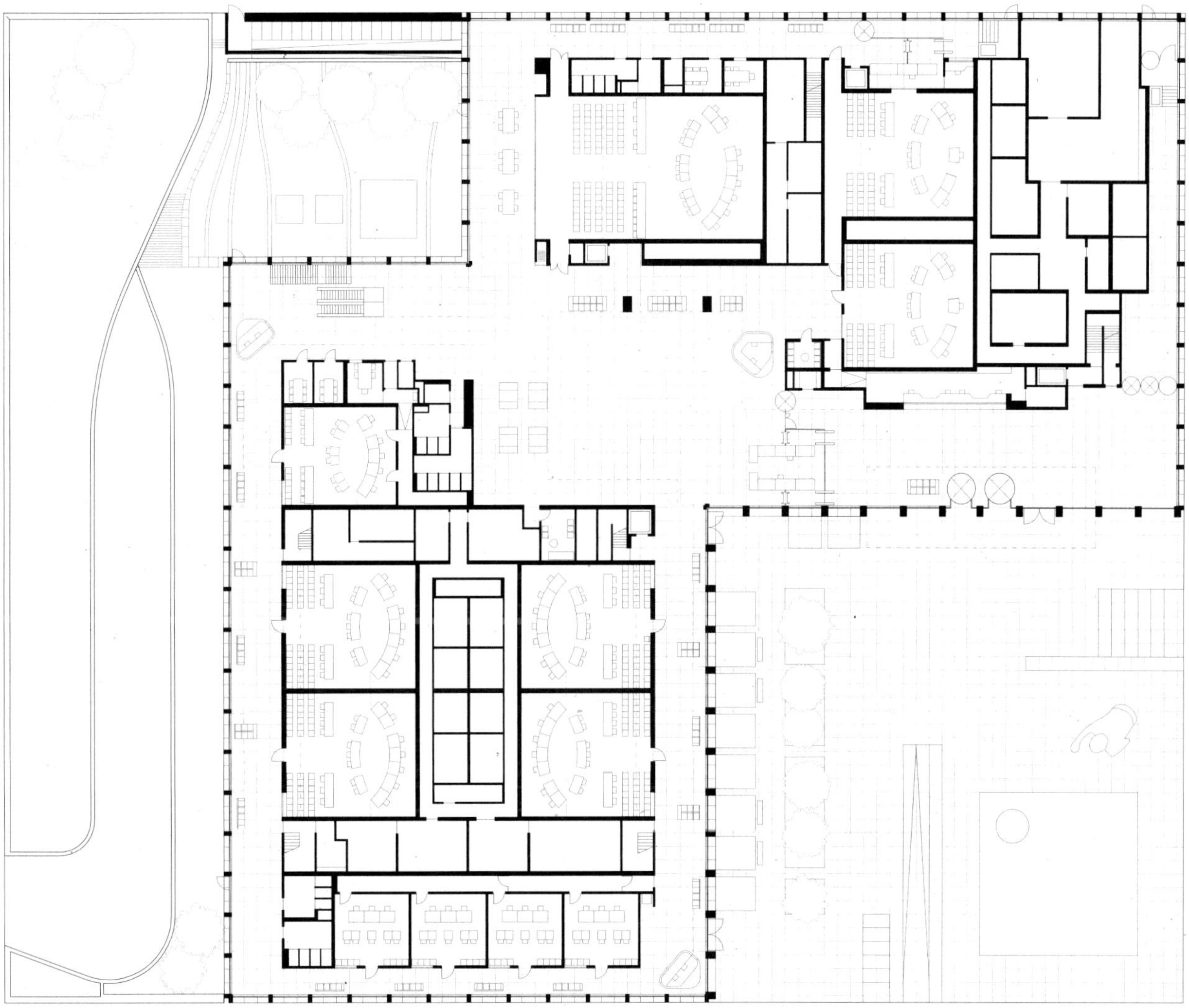

FLOOR PLAN 0

0 5 N

The courtrooms are the interior world of the Courthouse, not only figuratively, but also architecturally here. The architects have opted to place the foyers as intermediate spaces between this inner world and the city, and by doing so have given expression to the public nature of the administration of justice. Anyone can come to a hearing, though you are not able to see inside from a foyer. That would be disruptive. Yet daylight also reaches the courtrooms, albeit indirectly. The glazing next to the courtroom doors are opaque and continue the impression of marble cladding throughout the building. The transition from stone to glass is hardly noticeable. The opaque marbling only dissolves into transparency higher up where full light can enter.

The Court is an entity independent of the Public Prosecution Office. However, these two organizations deal with each other quite a bit, particularly in criminal cases. Prosecutors have their own counsel chambers joined to the courtrooms and their own work spaces in the building. The work spaces are part of the new 'tit for tat' policy and ASAP programme (to sentence offenders as swiftly as possible). From the outside these may appear to be hidden spaces, but in fact they are full of light and sightlines. The west face of the building, alongside the walled ramps for transporting detainees, has a sunken garden that brings colour and daylight into the basement level. Seven days a week, from 8 a.m. to 10 p.m., and opposite a decorative wall of climbing plants, lawbreakers can be given a swift sentence. This area also houses different rooms for things like arraignment, where the judge decides on the detention for the arrested person, and chambers where judges decide on pre-trial detention. There are also rooms where lawyers can counsel their detained clients.

In terms of organization, designing a courthouse is always a logistical challenge, but KAAN Architecten has managed to make a large organization compact. The architects have avoided a strict division of spaces by functional stacking and letting everything slot in logically under one roof. Its geometric simplicity, its balanced proportions and its natural accents have come to fruition through practical considerations and deliver a building that rises above the ordinary, while also simply serving everyday needs.

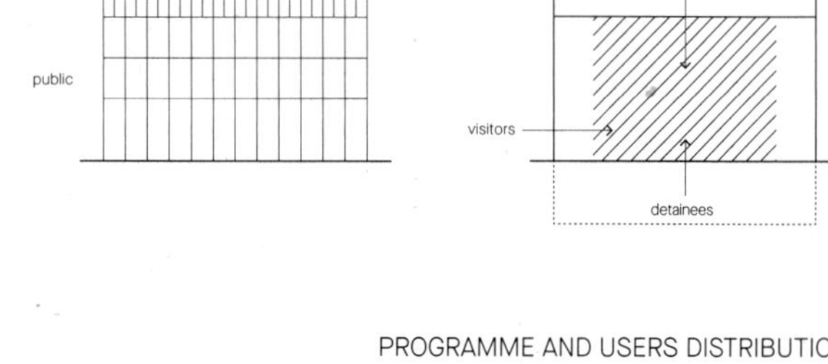

PROGRAMME AND USERS DISTRIBUTION

The uncluttered organization of the new Amsterdam Courthouse building is an ideal space for the clusters of visitors that come to the building daily. These range from 100 to 150 detainees with accompanying supervision, hundreds of staff and other professional visitors such as the press, and a colourful mix of other visitors from litigants, witnesses and defendants to victims of crime and accompanying parties. Victims are escorted and have access to a separate reception. This list speaks volumes about the required organization of a courthouse. If all these groups of visitors are able to find their way through the building in the absence of overbearing signage, then it says much about the quality of the architecture. You would have to have a particular talent for getting lost, if it were to occur in this building.

All staff and visitors can come through the entrance hall from the public square. The entrance canopy is low enough to prevent rain from blowing underneath. Once in the entrance hall, staff access their zone through a designated entry or they can go through the service entrance, the bicycle parking in the basement or the parking garage below, which is not open to the general public but reserved for staff or visitors by appointment. The north side is also where goods are delivered, such as the food for thousands of people. A little further up the street are the enclosed garden and the walled ramp for detainees. While walls may not conjure up pleasant images, seen from above they certainly do form an attractive sculptural meander.

SIDE ENTRANCE FOR SEPARATING VISITORS

The side entrance in the north facade is a special entry zone with tailored security checks for the public coming to watch courtroom proceedings in the specially designed gallery for the big cases that attract the public eye. The general public does not mingle with other visitors. A large sliding wall ensures these visitors are separated. This feature also removes pressure from the already busy foyers of other courtrooms and it means the extra-large courtroom can continue to be used when the rest of the building is closed (for example at the weekend).

The reception desk in the entrance hall directs people to the various foyer desks or to the Central Information Desk. Or perhaps a visitor has an appointment with a lawyer in the cafeteria. In any case, proceeding from the entrance everyone goes through security and enters the central hall. The compulsory security scan is a necessary interruption in the flow from public space to internal hall, but accessibility can only be guaranteed if security measures are in place. The entrance hall does, however, provide visitors with a view of the central hall and everything that unfolds there.

With 50 publicly accessible rooms, the new Amsterdam Courthouse has more rooms than the demolished complex had. They come in all sizes, from small, average, large and extra-large (for proceedings attracting a lot of attention). They are all furnished identically, with the exception of the art. The technical requirements are the same for all.

K
G
B

BODEBALIE
A

BODEBALIE
J
BODEBALIE
F

BODEBALIE K
G

BODEBALIE A

AMSTER

DAM

The courtrooms will see their fair share of tension and emotions, but the ability to hear all that is being said is paramount. Smooth walls would bounce the sound too much, and so the architects opted for fine vertical ribbing: this allows normal voice levels to travel evenly and softens the sound of raised voices. In criminal cases, the judge, prosecutor and defendant/detainee with supervision each enter the courtroom through their own passageway. The judges take their place behind a raised bench. Technology today requires a lot of wiring and this is hidden away in the podium under the bench. The mid-sized courtrooms have additional gallery seating for the public that can be accessed directly from the foyers. The back of the extra-large courtroom has a wide window that overlooks the enclosed garden.

All government funded building work allows for a small percentage to go to the artistic furnishing of the building. The showpiece in this regard is the tall statue on the square. In the sunken garden there are several sculptures by Jesse Wine, set on grey pedestals and against white gravel and vertical frames of greenery. The garden may be at basement level, but it is wide enough to bring daylight into this underground floor. Finally, some courtrooms feature work by Femmy Otten. While the furniture is the same in all the rooms, the art gives each its own individual feel. For example, the extra-large courtroom feels pleasant thanks to the two paintings of a rippling sea and a slightly overcast sky, placed opposite each other at different heights.

The building meets today's sustainability standards and can move with the times without having to undergo major renovation. Its durability is in no small part due to its built-in flexibility. We should assume that further digitization will mean future changes to a building, while this particular building must also retain its independent nature and public accessibility. On the office floors, a module of 900 millimetres was used throughout the design for facade, floor, ceiling and technical components. New walls can be placed or removed every 2,700 millimetres, and in the context of wide-open, column-free spaces this offers great flexibility. Most of the spaces in the office and transition zones can be easily converted into work spaces or meeting rooms. Spaces can also be easily joined: multiple rooms can become a conference room. Adding an extra storey on top of the building has also been anticipated.

The Amsterdam Courthouse by KAAN Architecten is an architectural achievement. It is a distinctly public building that cleverly embodies the public nature of the administration of justice. The pronounced volume of the building is nevertheless integrated into the context of its urban environment by way of its transparent facades and transitional square – features that also give it a dignified and welcoming face. Everything about the building feels relaxed and natural, as though its final form and spatial plan could not have come together in any other way. In Italian they have a word for this: *sprezzatura*, perfection that comes across as effortless.

II. Participating in Architectural Design

Construction is a very visible undertaking. Cranes, piles of building materials and groups of construction workers are a clear sign that a building plan is being executed. Yet building is also an invisible business. For example, without financing there can be no building. Or if a building permit is not granted, there will be no construction. There is a Dutch term for all the effort that goes into building: *bouwkolom* (the construction pillar). This economic term refers to all the parties involved in making a building happen. It spans everything from those involved in building regulations and interior design to demolition workers who set a new cycle of life in motion.

This construction pillar encompasses various chains and sub-chains. A client works closely with an architect, certainly when the client is also the future occupant, but also when this is not the case. Both must communicate with the city's urban planners about what they want to achieve. The planners work on behalf of the city council, the client works on behalf of the users and the architect works inclusively so that the voice of future users resonates throughout the design process. These voices can be a source of motivation, even of inspiration. This book on the Amsterdam Courthouse building provides a glimpse behind the scenes. KAAN Architecten posed a series of questions to those involved: the occupants of the courthouse, two professionals from the Central Government Real Estate Agency (*Rijksvastgoedbedrijf*, RVB) and the urban planners of the Zuidas, where the new building takes a prominent place in the urban landscape.

The following interviews were conducted by Marco Lanna of KAAN Architecten.

with HANS JANSSEN and ERIK TUIJP

All in the Service of Justice

KAAN ARCHITECTEN: Our design for the new Amsterdam Courthouse was based on the ambitions articulated by you as users of the building and by the Government Real Estate Agency (RVB) as commissioning party. We noticed immediately that one of the four keywords that the design of the building was to communicate was *gezagwekkend*, and that this couldn't be found in the dictionary. In one of the early information meetings, it was explained that the word is intended to express something like 'inspiring respect for authority' or for the authority of jurisdiction, without being overbearing or overwhelming. Indeed, that authoritative and inviting were the goals. How did the RVB, acting as representative of the future users, come to this non-existent term and how did it envision its realization?

ERIK TUIJP: It's a fair question and I completely understand why it piqued your interest. Why would we have to invent a word, when the Dutch language already has such a rich vocabulary. The reason is simple: what we were looking for didn't exist, neither in the dictionary nor in built form. We wanted a building that emanated authority, and was imposing to some extent, yet that also felt accessible to the public. Authority is important for the reputation of how justice is administered, but it shouldn't overpower the human aspect. We were looking for subtleties, things like your design proposed: raising the building and square just slightly from its environment to create an almost invisible kind of crash barrier, for example.

HANS JANSSEN: The word *gezagwekkend* ('subtly authoritative'), was coined by the then president of the Courthouse, Carla Eradus, who was brave enough to challenge the architects with a concept that would express a mixture of goals. Had we been able to draw, then we might have succeeded in visualizing the ambitions, but we have only words and demands at our disposal! What we absolutely did not want was something like the office towers in the neighbourhood. They are just there to be impressive and it doesn't matter what happens inside. Their architecture radiates prestige. For us, it's about radiating what happens inside, the workings of justice. It's not about us as an organization, but about those seeking justice.

Transparency and openness were elements we wanted to see and that you embraced in the design, since they prompt recognition and respect. Placing the courtrooms in the interior and having the foyers face outwards illustrates to the world what jurisdiction is really all about: ordinary people who come to court for justice. And this connection with outside provides them with orientation. The judges, on the other hand, remain internally focused, almost invisible except for those moments when they deliver rulings and when they use the transition zone or work upstairs in the offices, where they still have sufficient contact with the world at large.

KA: It sounds like what you were looking for in the new courthouse was primarily an expression of natural authority and something tangible and recognizable about how justice is served.

ET: Yes, and the forecourt plays a crucial role in this. It's the reception area of the courthouse and connection to the city.

HJ: The square is incredibly important, and we were impressed by this design feature for the site. It meets our needs because our mission as a courthouse is to remain close to the people, whether these are individuals seeking justice, professional staff or residents of the city. The square, which sort of functions as a new urban gateway in an area still under development, provided a unique opportunity to manifest this intertwining of society with the administration of justice in an outdoor and public setting. And the building stands out in comparison to the other buildings in the Zuidas. It's not just any old office block. It's smaller than the rest, but its sturdiness sets it off against the others and marks it as the only public building in the area. At the same time, it appears welcoming. The marble cladding draws you in to really look at it and it has a calming colour. The sightlines in and around the building are important, as is the integration with the existing built and planned environment. The organization and circulation inside is all very logical; just look at the central hall and the prominent position of Café Mokum on the first floor. As a visitor and citizen, it's easy to find your way around the building. The square and the building's open face on all sides make it instantly apparent that it is public space. It's robust yet friendly – a subtly authoritative building, just as we wanted.

ET: And the sculpture on the square, *Love or Generosity* by Nicole Eisenman, acts as a gatekeeper who subtly and kindly guides a visitor's entry.

KA: We've come to see a clear role for *Love or Generosity* in communicating authority and trust in the building. It's a 5-metre giant, so by definition imposing, but its bending and casual composure gives a welcoming feel. In the hands of the gender-fluid figure are an owl, arrow and acorn. It's reminiscent of the traditional representation of justice, of Lady Justice and her presence on older buildings of law.

HJ: We didn't ourselves conceive of the three symbols as representative of jurisdiction, the artist did that. The Art Committee that was involved in the development of the work of art accepted the associations related to these objects. Lady Justice speaks to the legal community: her scales draw our attention to the need for balance and the blindfold reminds us of our need to remain neutral. But we can draw a parallel between the giant gatekeeper and Lady Justice. The bronze symbols stand for wisdom, perseverance and progress. People come to the courthouse because they find themselves in a difficult spot or are unable to resolve a conflict, and what happens here should allow them to continue on with their lives. With these attributes, it's a work that fits here and gives visitors a sense of connection. As an organization we're glad *Love or Generosity* doesn't need an explanation. The artist herself came up with the title, which naturally conveys the friendliness of the piece.

ET: The three symbols indeed stand for the expectations visitors to the courthouse have. Rightly so, we expect the administration of justice to involve wisdom and to involve perseverance and progress in reaching justice. These are all qualities that we live and breathe in the building. Of course you expect justice to protect you from harm.

KA: These are high expectations that a court building must facilitate through its architecture and organization of space. In this regard, we noticed a certain parallel right from the beginning of the design process: while the administration of justice is one of the highest expressions of the democratic rule of law, it is ultimately carried out by people. The ancient accoutrements of masks and togas that once gave individuals a temporary authority and status within the community are still evident today in the robes worn in court. By wearing their robes, judges, prosecutors, court clerks and lawyers become more anonymous but also clearly represent their duties. Is it possible that, like the robe imbues an 'ordinary' person with a certain position and authority, the architecture of a building – merely a roof over public property – can impart a sense of authority where justice is administered?

HJ: The colour you chose for the facades does resemble the tone of our robes. However, I would prefer to highlight that this sense of neutrality and anonymity (also paralleled in the robes) is most clearly expressed in the courtrooms. These rooms are somewhat imposing for their high ceilings, but at the same time they are serene and reassuring. They provide privacy so those in the courtroom can remain anonymous to those outside. Yet there's also enough daylight coming in. The judges are positioned on a podium that distinguishes them from the others present, but the difference is not exaggerated. Everything has been meticulously designed to maintain a balance between authority, anonymity and humane interaction. This approach was applied repeatedly throughout the building, giving those in search of justice consistency.

ET: This is really at the heart of the functionality we envisioned. The courtroom is where it all happens, and everything else stands in the service of this. An optimal support system for the functioning of court processes wasn't simply a goal, it was a prerequisite that we communicated to the RVB, which was responsible for commissioning the building. Facilitating a case that comes to court is a logistical challenge, and the building's role is to lighten the load. That's what functionality is all about. In order to get a better picture of what a super-functional building might look like, we went through various exercises to develop descriptions of our primary processes, and these were handed over to the architects as part of the tender.

KA: The building's role is to serve. This statement seems so suitable to describe the functional character of the Amsterdam Courthouse, even though comfort is also not lacking. In what way does art contribute to this? The Courthouse has a large and valued art collection. And the collection has expanded with specific new works for the courtrooms, for example. Does

> *'For us, it's about radiating what happens inside, the workings of justice. It's not about us as an organization, but about those seeking justice. Transparency and openness were elements we wanted to see and that you embraced in the design, since they prompt recognition and respect.'*

the art enhance the atmosphere and the ability to make wise decisions or is it more a matter of contributing aesthetic quality, which helps our powers of concentration?

ET: Judges spend a lot of hours doing concentrated work, whether it's reviewing dossiers or listening to litigants in court. The works of art in and around the building – so also those in the courtrooms – are expressions of human imagination that can inspire good decision-making in difficult cases. It's not a form of distraction, rather an injection of new energy. This is true for everyone in the room, not just the judges.

HJ: The organization has been collecting art for about 30 years. It was started by a couple of judges who had a particular interest in art and wanted to do something about the dreariness of the old complex. The repetition at work and the long sessions can be quite tedious, and art is a way to break through the monotony. It's comparable to taking a little walk outside, getting a bit of fresh air. The collection has been carefully built from the start. Any art that feels confrontational or that inclines towards racism is avoided.

KA: As architects we put a lot of thought into the public part of the building – with good reason since it's the beating heart of the courthouse. Nonetheless, we imagine that achieving an optimal functionality in the upper part of offices and transition zone is not as straightforward as it may seem.

ET: The changes we'll encounter after moving in will be a big adjustment for the organization. For the first time we'll all be under one roof, which means we'll finally run into each other occasionally! The transition zone will be crucial in this respect. Arriving, meeting, researching, eating and drinking coffee together, discussing important business: all of these activities will happen here in an area that we didn't have before. The central location and meeting facilities of the Amsterdam Courthouse also make it a great venue for conferences for all the different courts in the country.

HJ: We're taking on a major challenge in the office area with multi-user work spaces, an entirely new concept for our organization. Preparing for a case is not like an average office job. For us, it's incredibly important to work in close proximity with your team. A totally flexible concept wouldn't work. So we've opted to work in fixed teams at fixed work stations, and that each team is responsible for enough flexibility to meet the 80 per cent workweek availability per work station, as set out by the current standards of the RVB. Secondly, a pilot project helped us discover that because of the high degree of concentration our work requires, the most sheltered type of flexible work space available for an office floor plan is the best option for us. The generous central zone you've been able to fit into the programme is a bonus. Once we get away from our desks, we're treated to a dynamic area with views to different floors, a space that is open to the outside world through generous windows, and room for finding your way and finding each other. So the comfort of a familiar work space hasn't been sacrificed.

KA: In your opinion, what was the key to achieving the objectives and creating a tailored, detailed building that supports all the processes of a courthouse?

HJ: Throughout the entire design process, we were able to participate and be involved in the decision-making on all aspects of the building – much more so than the provisions of the tender stipulated. We were able to look at the options for material choices, fixed and mobile furniture, installations and architectural details, not just to assess if they were pretty or durable enough, but also whether they would work and ultimately support the *raison d'être* of the building. Some elements were even examined by a broad range of organization representatives. This is unique to the approach of KAAN Architecten; others in a similar design contract wouldn't do this. It was only through this specific process that we were able to gain a building – and in particular courtrooms – that fully stands for and in the service of the administration of justice.

HANS JANSSEN is a board member of the Amsterdam Courthouse.
ERIK TUIJP is the programme manager for the building and also deputy judge at the Noord-Holland Courthouse.

Justice Needs to Be Seen to Be Done

with FOKKE VAN DIJK

> *'The democratic rule of law has been under pressure, felt to be less self-evident than before, and so it's important to reiterate it. Buildings are an engaging medium through which to exhibit how the rule of law functions. This is not a trivial ambition.*
>
> *...*
>
> *The building should visualize and support the role of the judiciary in society seems to me a basic functional requirement, or should at least be prioritized.'*

KAAN ARCHITECTEN: In today's society, feelings of fear, reticence, distrust and prejudice have to some extent replaced openness and trust. The unifying role and 'authority' of state institutions are often debated. And the safety of occupants and visitors to public buildings is a topic that is receiving a great deal of attention. What kinds of expectations were there for how the architecture should express openness and social values, while also not compromising on aspects of security and an optimal organizational capacity for court processes?

FOKKE VAN DIJK: As an important public institution, a rock conveying the rule of law, a courthouse deserves to be distinguished and approachable. This contributes to the visibility of the administration of justice, and therefore respect for the institution in society. Just the fact that people observe offenders being sentenced for their crimes confirms a sense of justice and strengthens their faith in constitutional democracy. English has a beautiful expression for this: Justice needs to be seen to be done. So visibility and recognition were concepts that warranted prominence in the design. And in order to achieve this, a sense of openness was paramount. People should feel free and welcome to attend hearings. At the same time, of course, it's a place where suspects and detainees are brought from the penitentiary, where emotions can run high and where violent incidents are not uncommon. This requires a lot of security, gates, scans and a complicated separation of judges, detainees and the public. Designing such a complex is a real challenge as it can easily turn into an insurmountable fortress. It is the task of architecture to resolve this paradox: providing accessibility along with security.

The design by KAAN Architecten manages to make a secure building feel like a user-friendly public place. The ample views from the square into the interior make for a welcoming approach. Raising the square to protect against ram-raiding meant unsightly and obstructive security measures like boulders and walls could be avoided. Lowering the entrance canopy to a human scale within the large grid of the facade gives natural direction, while not diminishing the almost imposing quality of the facade. Nicole Eisenman's work also softens the transition between scales. The balancing act itself – the balance between its aura, stringent grid, precision of execution and quality materials that speak of the historical continuation of the rule of law – is what supports and confirms the authority of the institution. This is exactly why we came up with the word *gezagwekkend*. A building has no authority, but it can evoke the feeling of authority. That's what this building does.

KA: That's the symbolic side of the story, but a courthouse is also big and has complex logistical requirements.

FVD: Indeed. Practical aspects, like minimizing the walking distance between the holding area and the courtrooms, directly affect how the building is organized. The time between calling up the defendant and arriving in the courtroom can be disruptive to the hearing. Separating the routes walked by judges, defendants and the public all too often ends up producing a labyrinth devoid of daylight and orientation. The legibility of a building for visitors also has a high functional value: an easy to understand route from the entrance through to the specific courtrooms reduces the workload of the information desk staff who otherwise have to keep giving directions. Efficiency shouldn't be confused with keeping things as small as possible. The ambition for the building was that its various spaces would be well-organized and composed in a very logical layout. All that space would then be worth it.

KA: Consortium NACH was awarded the contract to build the new courthouse, thanks in part to the design proposal by KAAN Architecten. However, the other teams also submitted interesting proposals. What were the most significant differences in the approach to the visibility of administering justice and having to accommodate security measures like separate circulation, which can pose a dilemma?

FVD: In general, designs submitted by consortiums for PPP-DBFMO projects set out by the RVB are always of a high standard. None of the submissions would have been out of place if realized. Of course there were individual aspects that scored differently. The design by KAAN Architecten scored very high on its integration in the urban fabric and a correspondingly appropriate architecture. This was the key difference. The design by Consortium Ido, with Hootsmans Architecten, Claus van Wageningen Architecten and Seville Peach, was almost the reverse of the design by NACH. Rather than an outdoor public space with blocks of courtrooms and offices in the interior, they opted for a hall of monumental proportions that spanned the centre, with the courtrooms and chamber attached to the facades. Functionally, this setup worked fine, but by putting a vast hollow space in the middle of the building, there was much less room for any kind of external gesture to the city like the forecourt by NACH. The third consortium with Jean Nouvel and Dam Architecten was terminated prematurely, so we can't really assess that design in the same way.

KA: Historically we can see an evolution in the architecture of government buildings for the three institutions of state: legislature, executive, judiciary. Until the nineteenth century, these buildings were most concerned with making their authority apparent, which often resulted in rather stiff and austere buildings that deflected any kind of interaction with people or city. Ornamentation was a complementary narrative that reinforced the distance between an omnipotent government and its citizens, like the effigy of Lady Justice with her blindfold, scales and sword on town halls and courthouses. The choice of materials was often borrowed from the architecture of previous bastions of power, like palaces, and was intended to inspire a sense of awe. The growth of democracy in Western Europe, certainly after the fall of Fascism and Nazism, completely turned the representation of government authority on its head. A new generation of government buildings in the Netherlands embodied communication with citizens, low-profile architecture and a reticence to employ any form of monumentality. Simultaneously, social engineering gained ground, for example by expanding the housing supply. This reticence in expressing the importance and authority of state bodies in society went hand in hand with a process of government withdrawal, which in the 1980s involved outsourcing responsibilities for government office buildings to property developers. In his book *The Future of the Netherlands* (2020), Chief Government Architect Floris Alkemade makes the case for the government to take back the lead. He notes the power of architecture to visualize a new future and to being a means of expressing a government's legitimacy in leading us to a sustainable future. So which goals should be given priority for the architecture of a prominent public building, circa 2021?

FVD: Your description of the trends is right. It's quite clear that the public stature, the prominent position in the urban landscape and the architecture of a courthouse are now more outspoken than the previous wave of the same typology. That's partly due to a new offensive approach: the democratic rule of law has been under pressure, felt to be less self-evident than before, and so it's important to reiterate it. Buildings are an engaging medium through which to exhibit how the rule of law functions. This is not a trivial ambition. The goals I mentioned in response to your previous question are all about being visible, approachable, authoritative and functional. That the building should visualize and support the role of the judiciary in society seems to me a basic functional requirement, or should at least be prioritized, if you prefer to describe it that way.

KA: Does the RVB also hope to generate public support over a longer period of time with this building? It's a little surprising that this new courthouse replaces an old one built less than 30 years ago.

FVD: We've learned some practical lessons from the past: by focusing primarily on efficiency and reduced construction costs, you end up building things no one feels any love for. Every building will need large-scale maintenance after some 30 years. The extent to which people are prepared to make the investment and accept the inconvenience of renovation, depends on the basic underlying quality of the building. Too much efficiency turns out to be counterproductive. There are historical, listed buildings for example, whose quality is so clear that we accept the limitations imposed by their architectural character, but this kind of quality was lacking in some of the courthouses built in the 1990s. The demolished Parnassus complex was also considered of lesser quality; functionally, spatially and technically it wasn't worth saving. With the new courthouses in Breda and Amsterdam we've tried to avoid this mistake. We hope to stretch the life of our buildings by going for extra-high ceiling heights, aspirational architecture and quality materials that won't feel worn out after a mere 30 years. And we ultimately hope to have made good choices.

FOKKE VAN DIJK is a senior architect at the Central Government Real Estate Agency (RVB)

An Unflinching Cornerstone in the Urban Landscape

with TON SCHAAP

KAAN ARCHITECTEN: The Zuidas area was already under construction when, more than ten years ago, the idea of thoroughly renovating the Amsterdam Courthouse complex started to gain ground. We know from our meetings with the RVB that they considered building a completely new courthouse at several possible locations in the city. Ultimately they decided to demolish and rebuild on the same site. From a logistical standpoint, this was a huge undertaking for the Courthouse as organization and for the RVB as facilitator. There needed to be a temporary building to house courtrooms during the construction phase and all the offices needed to be moved to nearby rental accommodations. If the courthouse had simply moved to a new location, the old complex could have continued to be used. What was the overriding reason to remain in the Zuidas?

TON SCHAAP: If you look at a map of Amsterdam, you can draw an ellipse with the Centraal Station and the Rijksmuseum as focal points. Within the ellipse are all the features that are unique to Amsterdam: its City Hall, Royal Palace with Dam Square, the Albert Cuyp market, the red-light district, department store De Bijenkorf, the Conservatorium and the Concert Hall. Accessibility and proximity are the reasons behind the clustering, but the ellipse is expanding. Train station Zuid is replacing the Rijksmuseum as new southern hub. It's happening, and it's also something we are seriously engaged in as urban planners. Rebuilding the courthouse in the Zuidas is part of this guided expansion. The search for other potential locations, done mostly confidentially, focused on the IJ-oevers area, where thousands of new homes, the new Palace of Justice and a range of cultural attractions are located. Centraal Station is now oriented in all directions.

The search ended with the decision to stay put, but this was indeed the most difficult option. It meant two major moves and a temporary courthouse. This saved the lawyers and accountants a lot of travel time, given that they had already chosen to work at this location.

The envisaged expansion of the ellipse also involved finding a place for all the law and accounting firms, and the Zuidas was the natural location. Adding the courthouse to the scenario was a logical step. KAAN Architecten used the corner site and its prominent position in the urban plan to their advantage by adding a forecourt to the building. The square connects nicely with one of the two other (leafy) squares in the neighbourhood that will soon serve as Station Zuid's entry zone. The open forecourt makes the Amsterdam Courthouse highly visible from all angles. Of course, its architecture also contributes to its visibility.

KA: Amsterdam is a city with a long tradition of liberalism and progress, and a place where generations of different cultures have come to live. How can the architecture of a courthouse contribute to the recognition and acceptance of 'authority' in a world of so many different backgrounds?

TS: The new courthouse has become an unflinching cornerstone in the urban landscape. In a city where power is always challenged and authority, as an accepted form of power, must repeatedly be earned, the new building has already achieved a natural command amid the din of the Zuidas. And this is thanks to its architecture, which combines a sense of transparency with a somewhat austere friendliness. The building offers the city its square – which may not be an intimate space, but it is accommodating and elegant – and the sense of public space continues fluidly indoors, into the hall and stairs, right up to the courtroom foyers. Upon leaving a courtroom after a hearing, the views of life out in the city are ever-present. In fact, coming back out is perhaps the best experience of this well-designed building, and symbolic too.

KA: The Zuidas district may now be the place where Amsterdam's heart – or maybe even that of the whole Randstad – beats the fastest for internationalization. What does a public building that represents an important form of democratic government need to distinguish itself from its neighbours – in a neighbourhood that has such a variety of people, businesses and architectural styles?

TS: The contrast between the measured grid of streets and the great diversity of architecture is what gives the Zuidas its distinct look and feel, in comparison with Berlage's adjacent urban plan to the north and the modernist district to the south. The former sports grounds alongside the A10 have become a high-density and multiuse neighbourhood. The architectural variety stems from the desire of builders to express an identity. Trends also feed the diversity: within two decades we've gone from 'corporate internationalism' to 'green pixels'. In terms of urban character, the variety is attractive because it puts the density into perspective and gives the pedestrian landmarks. We intend the Zuidas to be a district where the pedestrian and cyclist have priority, which, by the way, follows the current trend of walkable cities. Limiting the amount of through traffic also affords us the room to think about developing more green space. In any case, the two main north-south arteries, Parnassusweg and Beethovenstraat, connect the Zuidas with other parts of the city. So these two roads will ensure that the area starts to feel like part of Amsterdam.

The courthouse detaches itself from the 'branding' so prevalent in the architecture of the surrounding office buildings. In a way it's like a three-dimensional variation on the measured grid, rather than another new architectural statement next to all the others. In a quick glance you might even see a late work by architect Mies van der Rohe in the building, like from his American period. But instruments of design haven't been deployed as a reference or even as symbols, like columns and tympanums did in the past. They've been deployed for what they are: quality building materials that will last, and that in addition will guide and comfort users. Among these are the members of the staff, who have been provided with substantial spaces to work while still feeling contact with the city. The fact that a strong identity emerged from the process of designing everything in the service of something specific is the great lesson of this building. And the fact that a consortium of

'The building offers the city its square – which may not be an intimate space, but it is accommodating and elegant – and the sense of public space continues fluidly indoors, into the hall and stairs, right up to the courtroom foyers. Upon leaving a courtroom after a hearing, the views of life out in the city are ever-present. In fact, coming back out is perhaps the best experience of this well-designed building, and symbolic too.'

companies is responsible for maintaining the building for a few decades probably also helped because the result is real durability.

KA: The urban development concept for the Zuidas was all about creating lively streets. The ground floor programming was and is an important facet in this. The building lines on Parnassusweg (eastern edge) and Vermeulenpad (southern edge) had to have a minimum amount of building mass. Indeed, almost all the other Zuidas buildings make full use of their lots – in width, depth and height – and they make a sharp transition between indoors and the outside world. The need for a public square, as a place of significance within an urban landscape and as a forecourt to an important institution like a courthouse, was not something previously expressed in the Zuidas urban plan. Is there a reason for this?

TS: The master plan for the Zuidas grew out of an agreement between government planners and the municipality of Amsterdam, which included new-build, train and metro stations (Amsterdam Zuid), and a northern and southern tree-lined public square on top of two A10 motorway tunnels. The entire area was to become a new neighbourhood, and especially a unified one that was walkable and bikeable. The most important urban planning element regarding what's called the building envelope was a very clear entrance and an entrance positioned as closely as possible to the intersection of two significant spaces: Parnassusweg and the new Station Square. The DokDakPark raised walkway that will connect east (Minerva) and west (Britten) is still to be developed. The courthouse entrance needed to be clearly visible upon exiting the yet-to-be-built station. The station's square and street adjacent to the site were considered sufficient to accommodate the needs of the courthouse. So the site could be entirely built up as long all the other conditions were met. The idea was to keep the height as low as possible – building heights are always an issue in Amsterdam. The planned volume was almost cubic and, given the polarity of functions within a courthouse (from public service to private space for concentrated work), we envisaged a diagonal organization of space: so the 'most public' part would unfold near the entrance corner and the 'most closed' part would stretch towards the Roeskenstraat corner. The fact that the building was to have no backside and that it would be seen from all angles made for an interesting design challenge. Deliveries, parking for cars and bicycles, and secure passage for the transportation of detainees all had to be incorporated into the design and feel logical. The plan that won the tender had the surprising element of a square. KAAN Architecten came up with a great response to the 'most public' stipulation, and in doing so it solved a bunch of other issues as well. It was the reason why the proposal scored the highest. Other proposals included raising the site on a 5-metre plateau or filling up the entire site with building – and they were no match for your proposal. The indentation into the site for the courthouse square created more facades and therefore more opportunities for views, which were put to good use in the foyers outside the courtrooms.

KA: The immediate surroundings of the courthouse are still under construction. The Zuidasdok project will put the A10 underground and the aboveground space this creates will be open to slow east-west traffic (Mathijs Vermeulenpad, DokDakPark). The municipality is considering a long-term plan to lower the road on Parnassusweg. How will the courthouse and square be taken into account in a renewed network of public spaces?

TS: The new courthouse has revealed a previously unseen element: the ramp to the Strawinsky viaduct is suddenly and visibly an obstacle. The ramp is not only a hindrance to the sightline when coming out of the station towards the courthouse, it also makes it difficult to cross Parnassusweg. We can no longer ignore the serious decisions that need to be made about the Strawinsky viaduct.

The viaduct blocks the north-south sightlines on Parnassusweg. Clear sightlines are precisely the reason the ring road is being lowered at this point. As Station Zuid becomes busier and the surrounding area more dense, there will be an increased need for open spaces. The different modes of transportation will have to make way, and a walkable city will become more real. The northern square will be echoed by a southern pedestrian route: a raised green footpath from Roeskenstraat to Beatrixpark. Where this path nears the courthouse, it will connect to the new courthouse square. Then there's the question of what the long and wide viaducts on Beethovenstraat and Parnassusweg can offer us in terms of new space, once there's less traffic travelling under them. How can we pull these spaces into the city? Their locations are critical points in the whole. The flow between the courthouse square and Parnassusweg can then be improved, the throughway will become a street. The North-South metro line will extend to Hoofddorp, all international trains will stop at Station Zuid, thousands of new residential buildings will be realized, as well as office buildings. The one remaining (and best) building of the old courthouse complex will likely be turned into a museum for modern art.

KA: The stakeholders committee for the Zuidas decided to offer a financial contribution in support of the striking new work of art on the square. Why did they decide to do this?

TS: The realization of landmark works of art in public spaces is part of the Zuidas Vision. The municipality sees value in the focus that it brings to an area. A courthouse is one of a city's most important buildings, and the square of the Amsterdam Courthouse quickly became top of the list as a location for outstanding art. Participating in the hunt for an artist allowed us to exercise some influence in choices that affect the citizens of Amsterdam, choices that they would hopefully embrace. In this we were successful. The response so far has been tremendously positive. Nicole Eisenman's figure wishes you well as you enter the courthouse and seems to bend towards you in protection against all the high-rises. In more abstract terms, the bronze shapes contrast nicely with the stricter lines of the building and the scale of the piece mediates between the building size and the human dimension.

TON SCHAAP is an urban planner and supervisor of the Zuidas plans at the Municipality of Amsterdam.

with LOUISE ATTEMA

Quality, Now and for the Future

KAAN ARCHITECTEN: The new Amsterdam Courthouse is one of 15 buildings that was built on the basis of a PPS-DBFMO contract set out by the government. A 2016-2017 review of the DBFM(O) process by the Ministry of Finance draws a positive conclusion about this form of contracting. The stated benefits include financial advantages for the government, outsourcing risks to the consortium, assurances on performance, sufficient incentives for enterprises to deliver quality within a budget and timeline, and a high level of user satisfaction. What are the biggest positives in this form of tendering, in the experience of the RVB?

LOUISE ATTEMA: The RVB sees DBFMO more as a type of contract than a tender. Of course this type of contract also stipulates certain procedures, such as moments of dialogue, that contribute to achieving a high level of architectural quality. In general what we have noticed is that this way of working produces quality buildings without being prohibitively expensive. So a favourable price-quality ratio is a positive outcome. Quality at a reasonable price sits well with the government, especially for buildings intended to be used for a long time. Apart from the financial benefit, there's the focus on the user and the maintenance of the property (more so than in traditional, phased work). However, there are still aspects in the implementation of this type of contract that deserve our attention. For example, we often see in the operational phase that it takes a lot of time to coordinate the details of the contract, certainly in buildings with a special or complex use like a courthouse. Using DBFMO contracts is a way to unburden the RVB of detailed operations. Most issues regarding functionality are covered thoroughly during the dialogue phase and the subsequent design meetings, yet a good exchange of information between design team and operations team has proven difficult and time-consuming; the details of running primary processes are so complex. For buildings that are further into the operational phase, discussions about contractual conditions, deductions and changes suggested by the user continue to keep us busy.

KA: Has the RVB seen the role of the architect evolve in the time that DBFMO contracts have been used for government building projects? As architects, we see that what is asked of us within such a process is quite demanding compared with other work, which forces us to develop new skills. Is the RVB aware of this?

LA: In DBFMO contracts we look at projects through a long-term lens. The principal focus is quality and this will be determined by the architecture and functionality, both of which are influenced by the complexity of the organization's primary processes. Since quality is the decisive factor in awarding a DBFMO contract, the architect automatically exerts a great deal of influence on the bid. In fact, choosing the right architect is an essential factor for the consortium since it can make or break their submission. The architect's job within a consortium is much more varied, more lateral than usual, but increasingly they have been awarded the full spectrum of work. We just spoke about how important it is in DBFMO contracts to focus on use and maintenance. To achieve good results, things need to be anticipated early on in the design phase. Early collaboration between the operating and maintenance parties, on the one hand, and the architect on the other, is essential. All the designers involved must stay alert to the consequences of things like the choice of materials, the spatial organization of uses and the visibility of aspects that become important in the operations phase.

KA: The focus on quality and the role of the architect in the consortium seems

> *'In DBFMO contracts we look at projects through a long-term lens. The principal focus is quality and this will be determined by the architecture and functionality, both of which are influenced by the complexity of the organization's primary processes.'*

to me an interesting subject to explore in more detail. For example, since this project did not require a specific building volume on the site, it enabled us as the NACH team to first draw an optimum design and only then to optimize the details by working with a contractor. What does the RVB think of this process?

LA: I can understand the rationale. Involving a contractor early on can limit the potential to develop good solutions. Promising design elements are then stymied on the basis of very preliminary calculations and the focus of the design has to turn towards minimizing the square metres since the GFA (gross floor area) is the basis for cost estimates. This can lead to an impossible situation of trying to fit the whole programme into the available space. However, the opposite can also happen: a contractor comes to the table too late and is confronted with executing a seriously complicated plan. At the Amsterdam Courthouse we saw how the complexity of stacking functions and the use of different dimensions per stack led to a difficult construction phase with high time pressures. It probably couldn't have been done any differently at this location, certainly since it was the spacious square that won the contract, but this feature put a lot of pressure on the rest of the programme. Time will tell whether the quality we see now will last. In any case, it seems important to continue to seek the right balance between a certain design freedom for the architect and a smooth construction phase.

KA: KAAN Architecten has learned a lot in being party to a DBFMO contract. Performance is measured not just on the basis of what the architect has delivered upon completion, but on the durability of the design over the lifetime of the contract. And this encourages a design approach focused on creating a strong future-proof building. In addition, the length of the contract forces a client to think ahead about all the potential changes and unforeseen issues that could crop up during the life of the contract. This gets translated into a high degree of flexibility within the building. Spatial and organizational flexibility, together with robust and durable architectural and technical solutions, deliver a building that won't need a major overhaul in the future. This is incredibly important if we want to achieve a sustainable built environment. While DBFMO contracts have not yet incorporated the visibility of sustainable design as a priority, we can certainly say that sustainability gets built into our architecture. What does the RVB think about this, especially in relation to the sustainability that is generally sought in government buildings?

LA: Yes, the length of the contract really does force you to think about so many more aspects. We've already briefly discussed the attention the design phase must pay to details: that they should be durable, should age well, and be easy to clean and maintain. The architect will likely be constantly reminded of this in a DBFMO consortium. We are well aware that the most sustainable approach to a building is giving it the ability to accommodate changes in use without the need for demolition works. In this project, for example, we included a number of special requirements that strive to attain a maximum flexibility. The minimum 3-metre ceiling heights in the offices, for example, is exceptionally generous, but paves the way for other uses potentially being accommodated in the future. Anticipating the addition of an extra storey on top was another element. It's certainly the case that the building as it is today reflects the ideas and issues of a few years ago, when sustainability was not as hot a topic as it is now. The same tender or contract today would probably put more focus on an environmentally friendly design – or let's say: on communicating the green credentials of the building. But in a long-term, 30-year contract you also have the opportunity to work together on exploring sustainability goals as the market develops new green technologies and as government policies change. The obligation to keep exploring new opportunities is specified in the contract. Improvements can save money for both parties – the client and the property manager. And, of course, an existing relationship makes for smoother cooperation.

KA: The PPS-DBFMO contract for the design, construction, financing, operation and maintenance of the new Amsterdam Courthouse was accompanied by a very detailed brief (Output Specifications) that covered everything. We can well imagine that drawing up this document was a team effort and that it involved a lot of explorative research. Did the RVB draft a spatial concept or functional master plan in order to develop specifications?

LA: Fokke van Dijk is the best person to answer this question, since it touches on his expertise and his role in the project.

FOKKE VAN DIJK: The RVB is responsible for developing a realistic building commission. Of course the RVB architects do studies and sketches in the preliminary phase to test the viability of some points. The required degree of precision and elaboration differs per project. Certainly when there are many constraints around a project, you need to make things concrete more quickly and the drawings become more prescriptive. Consider, for instance, listed buildings or complex building conversions where a new programme has to fit into the existing framework. An accurate assessment of the feasibility is necessary to determine the potential of the project. The large new-build site for the Amsterdam Courthouse did not need such in-depth studies. The RVB regularly works on projects dealing with the judicial branch, so we are familiar with the different archetypal functions and at an abstract level we can reasonably assure a Courthouse management board whether their programme will fit the location. For the Amsterdam Courthouse site it was enough to develop a scheme for the spatial relationships, and we left the rest up to the creativity of the market. In urban planning terms, we did put a lot of time and energy into how the building would integrate. Creating space for the square was not a given for the municipality. We also studied at length the preconditions for creating an acceptable building mass precisely where the Zuidas district transitions into the smaller scale residential neighbourhood on the northern edge. Finally, the location on the edge of the Zuidas, which up until that point was primarily seen as a business district, was not an obvious choice for the board, especially given its ambition for a more prominent position in the city. Anchoring the building in the surrounding public space therefore received a lot of attention.

LOUISE ATTEMA is a project manager at the Central Government Real Estate Agency (RVB).

III. DBFMO: Good Architecture Is Paramount

PPP-DBFMO contracts are Public-Private Partnerships that encompass the Design, Build, Financing, Maintenance and Operations of a structure, whether this a building, bridge, road or waterworks. It may sound complicated, but the basic principle behind it is very simple: getting something done by a professional without fiddling about with it yourself. You do the same when it comes to a Dutch croquette: you buy it frozen from a quality delicatessen or from a supermarket, but always the good brand, because you do have your standards. Of course, the actual implementation of a DBFMO contract is not as simple as the principle.

For any large building project the Dutch government will seek collaboration with a consortium, a group of firms that together form a balanced team of experts. The consortium becomes the single point of contact, the body that is contractually responsible for organizing everything, taking on the risks and delivering it all on time. Quite simply, the government commissions a cooperative party to execute a project, and this transaction is subject to European procurement and competition rules, which means tenders go out and bids come in – and it all has to run smoothly. The buyer's demands must be comprehensive and crystal clear because the interests at stake are huge. Leadership in running the project must be exemplary.

Kees Kaan and Vincent Panhuysen were the lead architects of the Amsterdam Courthouse, and here they explore the question of how architects work in such a project. With their experience in Amsterdam, and also in building the Supreme Court of the Netherlands in The Hague, they are able to share some intelligent observations.

KEES KAAN and VINCENT PANHUYSEN

DBFMO: Good Architecture Is Paramount

When traditional tendering is replaced by a PPP-DBFMO contract, what does this mean for the architecture, or in other words, for the art and skill of designing buildings? The responsibilities of this kind of contract range from designing for smooth construction to designing for healthy catering. In our work on two major courthouse projects we have come to see how the architect is the pivotal figure in a PPP-DBFMO contract. But this pivotal position very much depends on intensive cooperation with engineers and other parties outside of the D of Design. For instance, the design must also show partners how easy the M of Maintenance will be in the future.

Before we elaborate, let us first make a confession. When we first heard of a PPP-DBFMO contract, and a project manager who had worked at the Central Government Real Estate Agency (*Rijksvastgoedbedrijf*, RVB) explained to us what it involved, we were pessimistic. We believed that it would mean a loss of creative control. After all, such a wide-ranging and complex contract could only be pursued by big players, and that meant the big construction firms. It was our impression that the architect would then definitively be relegated to the background, acting as a sort of subcontractor in the service of the construction company. It seemed that the state, in accordance with neoliberal ideals, was withdrawing even further from its public and social responsibilities.

However, our fears were unwarranted. In practice, there is room for the architect to turn the tables, or in other words, to play a decisive role in winning a tender. State-run tenders always demand quality architecture, and this includes high functionality and sustainability. Good architecture is paramount and it is precisely this that can win a contract. In a state tender, the specifications are what in a commercial context would be called the client brief – though there is a difference because the specifications do not prescribe how things should be made, but rather why they are being made. For instance: they stipulate that there should be sufficient capacity to wash hands, but not how many sinks are needed? this will take. This gives an architect a great deal of freedom. In a more typical situation, the architect competes for a contract, but is not privy to construction decisions or other issues as they are kept out of his or her hands. In contrast, in a PPP-DBFMO tender, in which a variety of products and services are amalgamated, the emphasis is on the functional relationship between a building and its workings.

This difference also has other consequences. In a traditional situation the value of a contract lies basically in the architect's hourly fee. The net value of a tendered contract, from design and build to all services up to and including operation (in this case, a 30-year operation timeframe) is many times the hourly fee. This can be won if you design a good building. The one qualification is that the design must come to fruition through the input of skilled professionals in the consortium and offer the best possible integration of functions. The selection criteria and the assessment process are crucial. The government seeks maximum value for money and that money is limited to a set budget. It will always be about the best quality-price ratio, and not the cheapest option, otherwise the PPP would fall apart.

Tendering involves several roundtable discussions with the commissioning party. A number of consortiums compete over a span of 15 to 18 months as they design and develop their ideas, moving towards the best possible bid. Near-definite designs are carefully guarded secrets until the moment when the so-called BAFOs (Best and Final Offers) are put on the table.

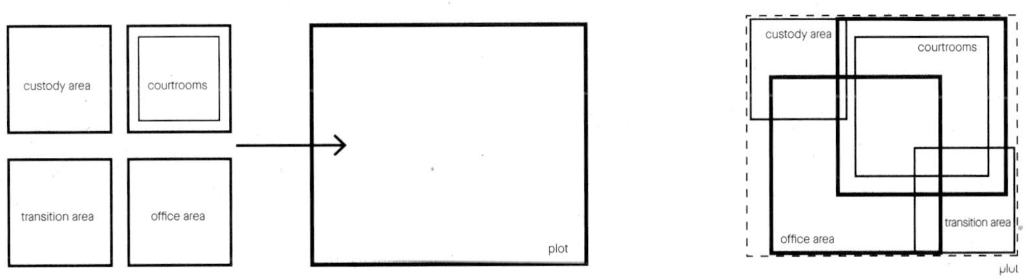

THE COURTHOUSE'S FUNCTIONAL PROGRAMME PROJECTED ONTO THE SITE

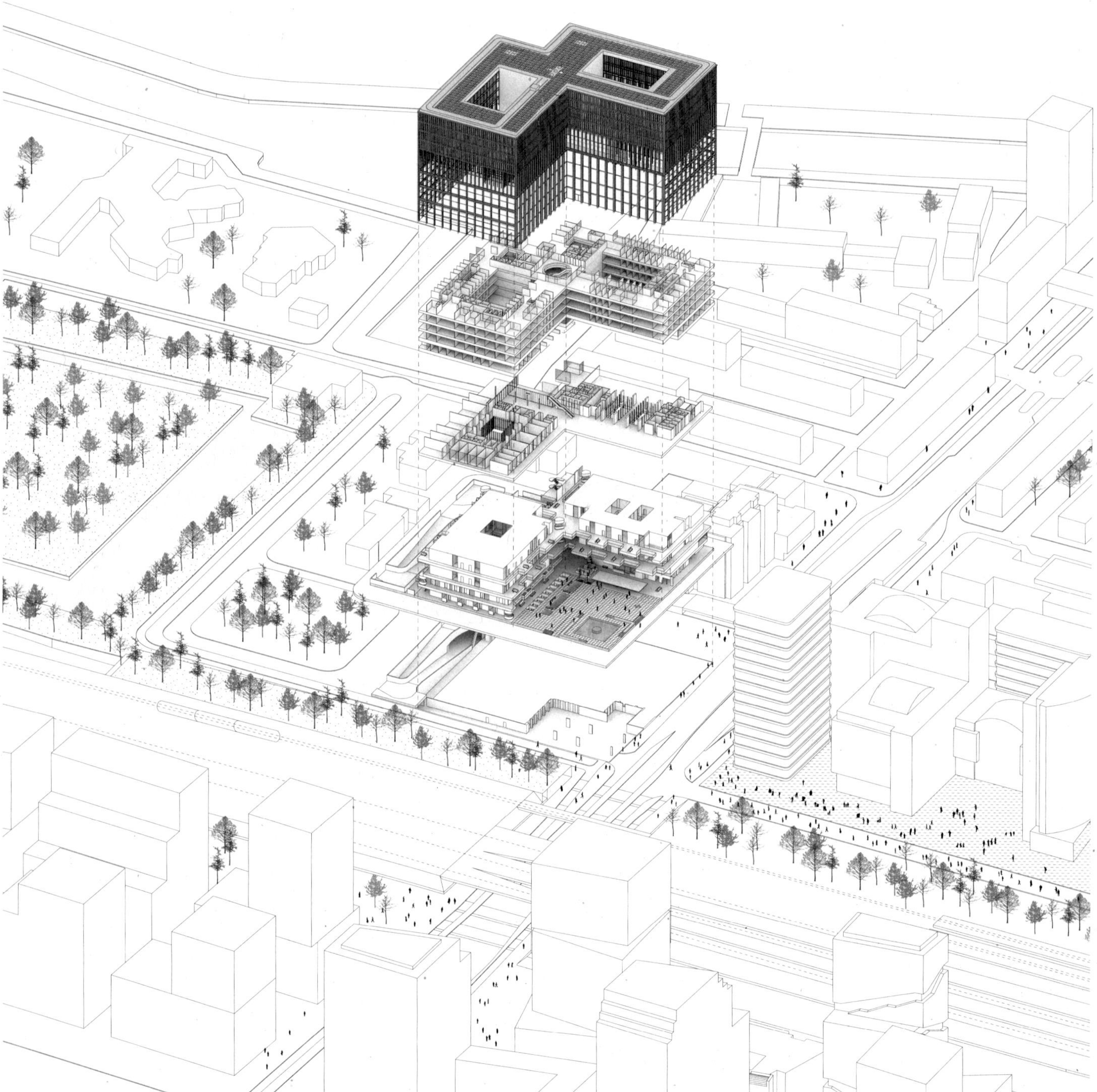

The winner can now be held accountable for promises made. It's a fantastically exciting and exhilarating process. The discussions provide clear feedback on preliminary designs. The operations professionals provide input on functionality, allowing us to find an optimal ratio between investment costs and operating costs, which makes the design process more interesting and inevitably leads to sustainable ideas. It's not just about delivering an empty building for a certain point in time, but delivering a design that meets user needs, is ready with facilities, interior furnishings, energy plans and other operational aspects, and is basically future-proof.

The engineering, construction and future development of the end-product are all taken into account. A BAFO design must be feasible down to the smallest detail. It is a question of integrated design. The builders and engineers work together from day one in search of the best (again, not the cheapest) solutions to the issues that crop up or may emerge in the future. Installations, user facilities, security and safety, sustainability, greenery, circulation. . . it's all considered in the making of the design. On the whole, it's not unlike industrial product design. And it is all possible thanks to the integrated software of BIM, a computerized representation of a complete building that makes the consequences of alterations immediately visible.

This approach and the procedures involved require the architect, more than ever, to assume a leading role. After all, the design is the guiding force. All the information and discussions are visualized in scenarios in order to make balanced decisions in the context of the greater whole. The greater whole is the design narrative, and the storyteller is the architect.

Allow us to explain this notion of a narrative – while also first noting that it's not about image or feel, or a superficial face, or individual architectural interpretation. A narrative is a governing organizational principle, a way of moulding a new building. Much depends on considering and applying the narrative effectively. The impressive public space of the Seagram Building in New York by architect Ludwig Mies van der Rohe was the result of how everyone working on the skyscraper believed in the narrative: give the city a plaza by setting the building line back from the urban grid. It was an unprecedented decision.

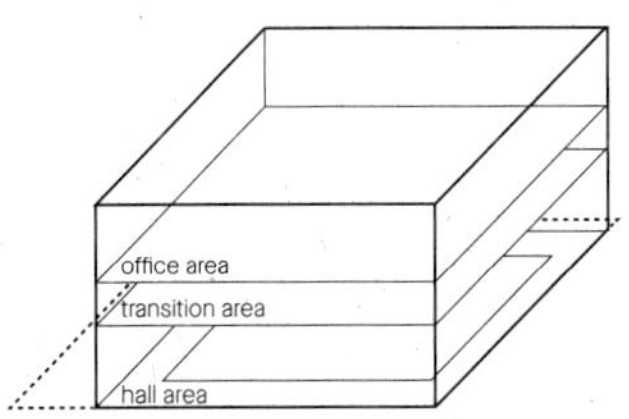

FUNCTIONAL STRATIFICATION

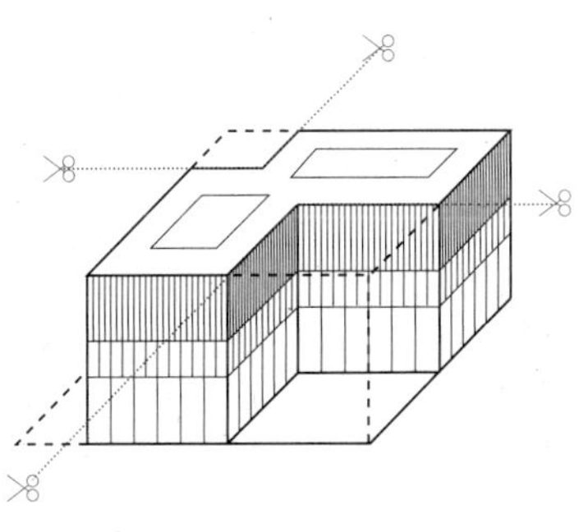

FORECOURT AND GARDEN COURTYARD CUT OUT OF THE URBAN BLOCK

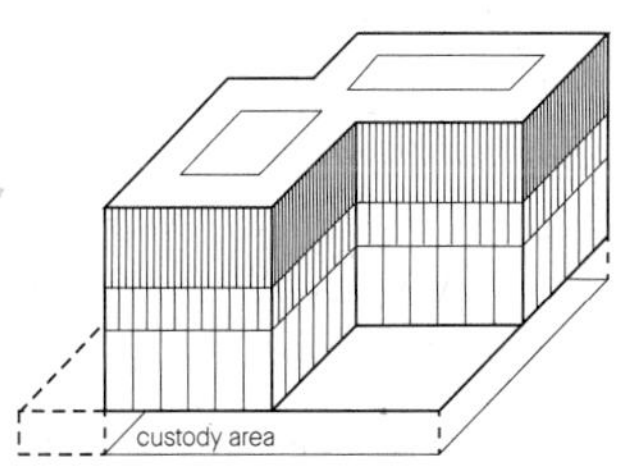

CUSTODY AREA AT LEVEL -1

If a client and occupant, in this case the RVB and Courthouse management, express a joint ambition for the new building to be highly visible and easily recognizable as a courthouse, then we follow up with a question: What exactly should stand out and be so recognizable? The open, public character of the building and the closed, defensive nature of its security (which makes the openness possible) will already have an inherent form of expression, a shape and stature, a face. A narrative or shared theme is needed to bind the interests of all those involved in the project. Each professional through the design, execution, operation and maintenance phases needs to connect with and support the narrative. As architects, we initiate the narrative. For the courthouse it was that the administration of justice is a public affair and as such it stands in the middle of society and takes place in front of our eyes. So on the one hand, the courthouse is a distinguished public institution and, on the other, a dignified everyday place. This is what prompted all the openness and transparency, the sightlines into and out of the building on the public ground floor. In addition, we also believe that a building must contribute something to its surroundings, be durable, and be comfortable in use.

That is one part of the narrative. A bigger part of the narrative concerns how everyone involved, each contributing their expertise to enhance the project, comes to the envisaged architectural expression while also meeting functional demands. Again, to use the Amsterdam Courthouse as an example: a quarter of the site was given over to a public square as part of our efforts to weave the building into its urban context, and the consequences of this choice meant the holding area for detainees would move down a level, below the ground floor. It was also important for this not to cause negative consequences elsewhere in the building, just as placing the courtroom foyers directly behind the facades should not disadvantage other spaces in the building. A PPS-DBFMO contract provides room for this experimental shifting since it only stipulates the needs the building must serve and the rules it must comply with, and does not prescribe how these demands should be met. Yet how can everyone come to an agreement on what's right? This can only happen if everyone is striving to achieve the same narrative. The narrative is the driving force.

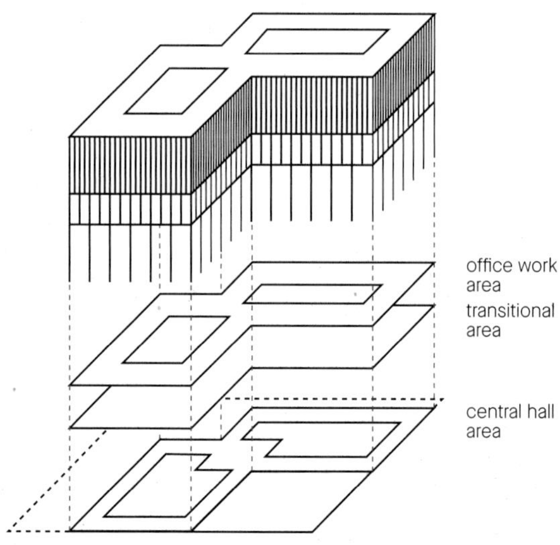

THE FACADE'S DIVISIONS MAKE THE FUNCTIONAL LAYERING VISIBLE

'When we follow the chosen narrative, we are creating exceptional value. The project rises above each individual contribution. The whole is many times greater than the sum of its parts.'

It is fascinating to see that the design doesn't simply serve as a model to execute, a model for a possible future. The model is also a means to mobilize forces, a vehicle for cooperation. The Amsterdam Courthouse is special to us because we encountered the right set of circumstances. Prior to the tender, a group of professionals had come together and each had their own ideas on the best working process and the right moments for input from the various disciplines. The precise composition of the team that formed the consortium New Amsterdam Court House (NACH) was actually quite special, and thus instrumental in the success.

All the partners had experience in tendering and the same goals in mind: doing things differently and learning from past mistakes. The collaboration and the space given to each discipline was exceptional. Nobody spoke out of turn. It was a stimulating experience and an intelligent working process. Architects, managers, engineers, finance experts, builders, facility managers – they all had the same mission in mind. Working together is only fun when it leads to success. Without it, collaboration quickly turns into resistance. Team members have to be able to trust each other blindly, so that everyone can concentrate on their own tasks and not get lost in trying to control other aspects. Individual performance then counts for everything.

A building constructed in partnership under a DBFMO contract is the outcome of an invigorating team effort, more so than when a building is designed to meet the desires of a client brief and then contracted out for construction. The notion of a *Gesamtkunstwerk* automatically springs to mind. Though not an entirely accurate term, since it refers to a fusion of different arts such as when music, dance, poetry, costumes and stage design come together in opera, it does express a combination of talents. Given the successful fusion of disciplines and the successful end result, the creation of a *Gesamtkunstwerk* has unquestionably been accomplished.

IV. Seemingly Effortless

In this chapter we take you on a journey through the architectural elements of the building – as seen on the computer screens of KAAN Architecten. It illustrates how the courthouse took shape and all the effort that goes into creating a successful building.

The Amsterdam Courthouse seems to have come into being without much effort, as though born fully formed. How do you design and build something so that it appears both natural and exceptional – natural in the sense of a good fit and exceptional in its execution and ability to stand out? Below, a few themes are highlighted and accompanied by explanations: the facade in relation to the concepts of friendliness and formality, the courtrooms as expressions of the heart of the matter, and the necessary ramps as a sculptural weave. The building and how to navigate it come across as self-evident, but these highlights make clear that no effort was wasted. From massive volumes to fine details, a well-formed and eloquent building can only speak to us if it is founded on skill, expertise and discipline.

It should be clear that prior to any building being built, it lives as a design – one that is more than simply a drawing with fixed lines. The spirit and feel of the building is, however, predetermined. For the Amsterdam Courthouse the guiding principle was that the administration of justice is a public affair that confirms the rule of law and is part of everyday life. The tone of the courthouse is set by a few harmonizing factors: a public square spanning a quarter of the site, the expansive public reception space, and the large windows giving views into and out of the building. In other words, the building creates a 'narrative' with and for the public.

The following chapter was compiled by Marten Dashorst of KAAN Architecten.

Facade

KAAN Architecten believes a courthouse should communicate the validity and normalcy of jurisdiction in a public place. Ideally, there would be no separation at all between the interior of a courthouse and its surroundings. Practical considerations such as security and weather conditions make walls inevitable. These walls are the facades we read upon approaching the building, and they offer plenty of visibility and views.

GLASS

Between the loadbearing columns of the facade, it is all glass. There are no rebates and no visible frames in the structural glazing. The laminated glass panes are as big as it is possible to manufacture in Europe and the setting of the glass was meticulously orchestrated. There are minimum requirements for glass regarding light transmission factors (LTF) and burglary protection (Resistance Class), and within this range the architects chose double-glazed panels of 8-14-10 mm that limit the total solar radiant heat gain to 34 per cent and the reflection of light to just 13 per cent. This almost totally eliminates distracting reflections. An extra special sun-filtering foil was selected to minimize the greenish coloration of the glazing. The choice of glass was important to maintain the transparency of the interior spaces under all light conditions, such as for the foyer spaces outside the courtrooms. Equally as important, however, was minimizing the need for indoor blinds, even though this is unavoidable in some cases. The architects were able to convince everyone involved that maximum transparency could go hand in hand with optimal comfort: by doing detailed studies of sun angles and shade in the foyers, simulating the indoor climate with Computational Fluid Dynamics (CFD) and orientating the furniture appropriately.

FACADE PILASTERS

The steel columns of the facade protrude away from the glazing on the outside, leaving the glass seams on the inside flat and smooth. This is true from the ground floor all the way through the foyer corridors and up to the upper floors of the offices. The skeleton of the structure consists of steel I-beams wrapped in quality insulation and sturdy, dimensionally stable metal casings. The columns of the two facades facing the square are clad in stone up to the transition zone at 23 metres. These marble pilasters have been kept to a minimum width so as to open up the building's face as much as possible. And the glazing in between has been slipped into the flanges of the steel beams, avoiding any unsightly joints.

This all sounds easy, but the detail necessary to make it happen is astounding. Structural movement, a calculation of tolerances, and production alterations – these were all studied in detail. The I-beams were adjusted for greater strength and given a shorter inner flange while offering just enough contact with the indoor temperature to prevent distortion. When sawing off the inner flanges, the lost tolerances were immediately corrected to less than 10 millimetres, which is quite exceptional for 23-metre beams. During construction, the tolerances were constantly monitored and the entire supporting structure was measured again for the proper installation of the metal casings over top. The new measurements were used to correct all the casings individually so that a near perfect fit was achieved.

Within this carefully thought-out system for a quality facade, the two columns at the inner corner of the building deserve special mention. These columns were not originally included in the structural design, which suited the architectural vision of a transparent building over the diagonal line between the square, central hall and enclosed garden. When it became clear that the heavy loads at this inner corner needed a supporting column, the design research focused on solutions that would not disrupt the visual relationships along this diagonal. Remarkably, after many drawings, the best column shape turned out to parallel the ratios of the building's ground plan: a 500 by 500 millimetre square with two corners cut out (smaller squares of 250 and 125 millimetres). The glass panes and the floor edges, already detailed with a metal profile finishing to bring the floor flush with the steel

columns, would slot into this shape perfectly. Yet from a structural point of view, combining standard steel beams to get the desired shape would not be sufficient to support the load. In the end, it was decided to weld together steel plates with a thickness of 45 millimetres. Although this welding was predicted to cause a 40 millimetre distortion of the whole under higher temperatures, the largest actual measured deformation was limited to 25 millimetres.

FACADE CASINGS

The steel column casings are made of factory-welded steel sheets with a thickness of 5 millimetres. The choice of steel instead of aluminium – considered as an alternative – was due to the large dimensions of the steel columns. Aluminium comes in smaller panels, and so the seams would have detracted from the unified appearance of the whole. It was vital to achieve smooth surfaces and sharp corners in manufacturing the steel sheets. The relatively thick sheets also ensure tighter tolerances and a straighter, more stable construction. Deformation during welding was kept to a minimum by constantly angling the beams slightly. For this purpose, the manufacturer developed an innovative monitoring system. Shorter structural beams, less load and less insulation on the upper floors made it possible to taper the column casings from 350 millimetres in the substructure to 300 millimetres on the office floors. Although practically imperceptible, this means more daylight for the upper office floors.

At the second, third, fifth, seventh, eighth, ninth and tenth storeys, the columns are connected horizontally. These horizontal elements are capped by metal casings with a bevelled upper edge, and on the upper floors of the offices extra verticals were added to these casings, not for extra support but to give the facade a rich sculptural relief. The architects encountered two challenges in mounting the casings in a way that would sustain the desired aesthetics.

First, while the casings had to be secured to the steel, the attachment also had to remain invisible and allow for future access. The undersides of the casings were therefore fitted with interior hinges. It took quite some effort to determine the exact position of the hinges and clamps, since the initial trials showed too much welding work on the outside. Second, the seams in the casings (both horizontal and vertical) were thoroughly analysed and specially designed: they had to meet precise demands at different points in the building, for aspects like greater temperature differences, greater distortions due to longer casings, and the ability to anchor the construction hoist during placement and replacement. During the design process, the most sensitive spots were identified and, subsequently, the other seams were assessed and detailed in order to unify the whole. In general, the horizontal seams of the column casings are slightly wider than the vertical ones of the columns, but because a facade is always viewed from below, this difference is practically imperceptible.

FLOORS

Most of the facade columns also support the floor beams that run under the foyers. These connection points are encased by metal flashings in the same colour as the steel surrounding the glazing. The gaps between floor and glass were dimensioned to allow cleaning access and enough space for air flow to regulate the temperature at this sensitive point between indoors and outdoors: too much temperature difference and the glass can crack. Where the floor beams connect to the columns they were also trimmed to ensure a clean marble floor line running the length of the facade. Where there are double-height spaces along the facade, a sturdy

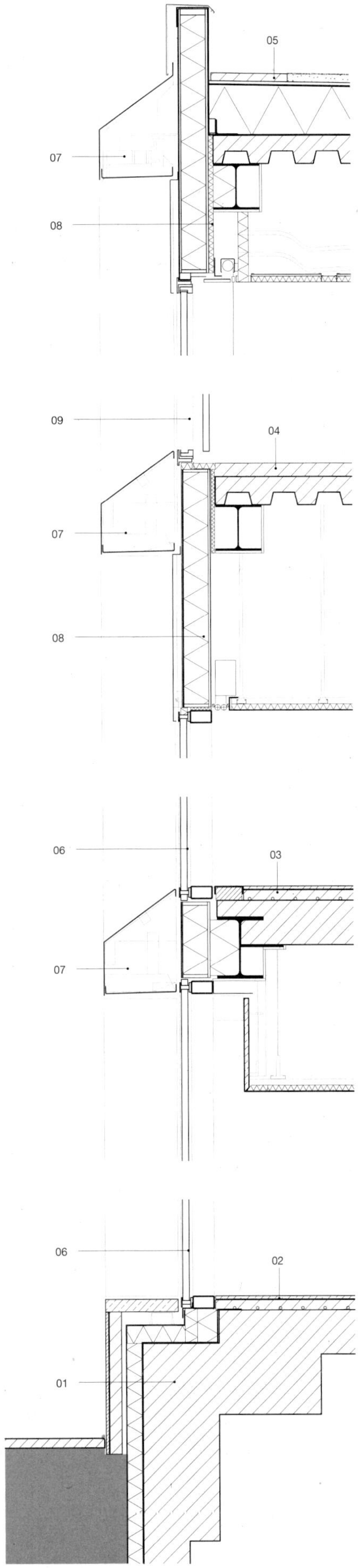

DETAILED FACADE SECTION

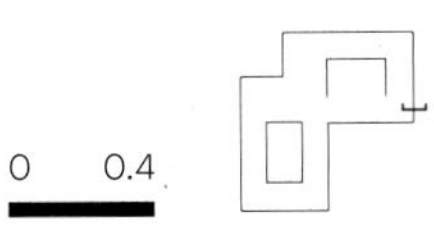

01 base (outside-to-inside)
- marble, polished: grain 220;
- prefabricated concrete element, mounted to concrete wall;
- bitumen waterproofing membrane;
- resol insulation, λ = 0,018 W/m.K, incl. aluminium foil facing;
- bitumen membrane base layer;
- concrete wall, cast-in-place;
- marble cover plate on top of plinth, thickness: 80mm

02 ground floor
- marble, 1200×1200mm, glued to screed,
cement joints, 3mm, grey, washed, polished, grain 220;
- cement screed layer with underfloor heating and cooling;
- monolithic concrete floor;
- dust binder coating;

03 foyer floor
- marble, 1200×1200mm, glued to screed,
cement joints, 3mm, grey, washed, polished, grain 220;
- cement screed layer with underfloor heating and cooling;
- monolithic concrete floor;
- steel structure, clad with fire protection board;
- ventilation plenum
- acoustic plaster, seamless, on mineral wool, white;
- alcoves: marble, polished: grain 220,
hidden mounting with anchors, open joints 8mm to assist plenum ventilation;

04 office floor
- carpet tiles, 500×500mm;
- cement screed layer;
- composite steel-concrete floor;
- steel structure, clad with fire protection board;
- acoustic plaster, seamless, on mineral wool,
colour: RAL9010, glossiness 30%;

05 roof
- sedum roof, filter mat, drainage buffer, protection and absorption layer;
- bitumen waterproofing membrane, provided with root and rhizome inhibitors;
- C-EPS screed mortar;
- emergency bitumen membrane;
- composite steel-concrete floor;
- steel structure, clad with fire protection board;
- activated climate ceiling, with perforated panel elements and solid line elements, steel, powder coating: RAL9010, glossiness 30%,
inlay: mineral wool and black filter facing

06 foyer facade
- steel curtain wall, rectangular box section transoms 140×80mm
vertically mounted to main load bearing structure
- glazing: 4.2.4 - 18A - 8.2.8
LTA: 67%, g-value: 0,34, reflectance: 13%

07 horizontal facade element
- folded steel sheet element, 3mm, coating: finish layer: RAL8022, satin;
- hidden mounting to steel column cover element
- topside angled ca. 35 degrees;
- underside hinged to assist with mounting and glass replacement

08 closed facade element (outside-to-inside)
- aluminium cassette element, 3mm, powder coating: RAL8022, glossiness 30%;
hidden mounting with conversion brackets;
- timber frame parapet element:
breather membrane, waterproofing,
pinewood plywood, 12mm,
glass wool insulation, λ = 0,018 W/m.K,
I-beam 45×160mm,
vapour control layer,
OSB, 12mm,
steel sheet element, galvanised, 3mm

09 office facade
- aluminium window frame, powder coat: RAL8022, glossiness 30%
provided with hidden window leaf with vertical hinge;
- glazing: 8 - 20A - 6.4.6,
LTA: 68%, g-value: 0,34, reflectance: 13%

DETAILED HORIZONTAL FACADE SECTION

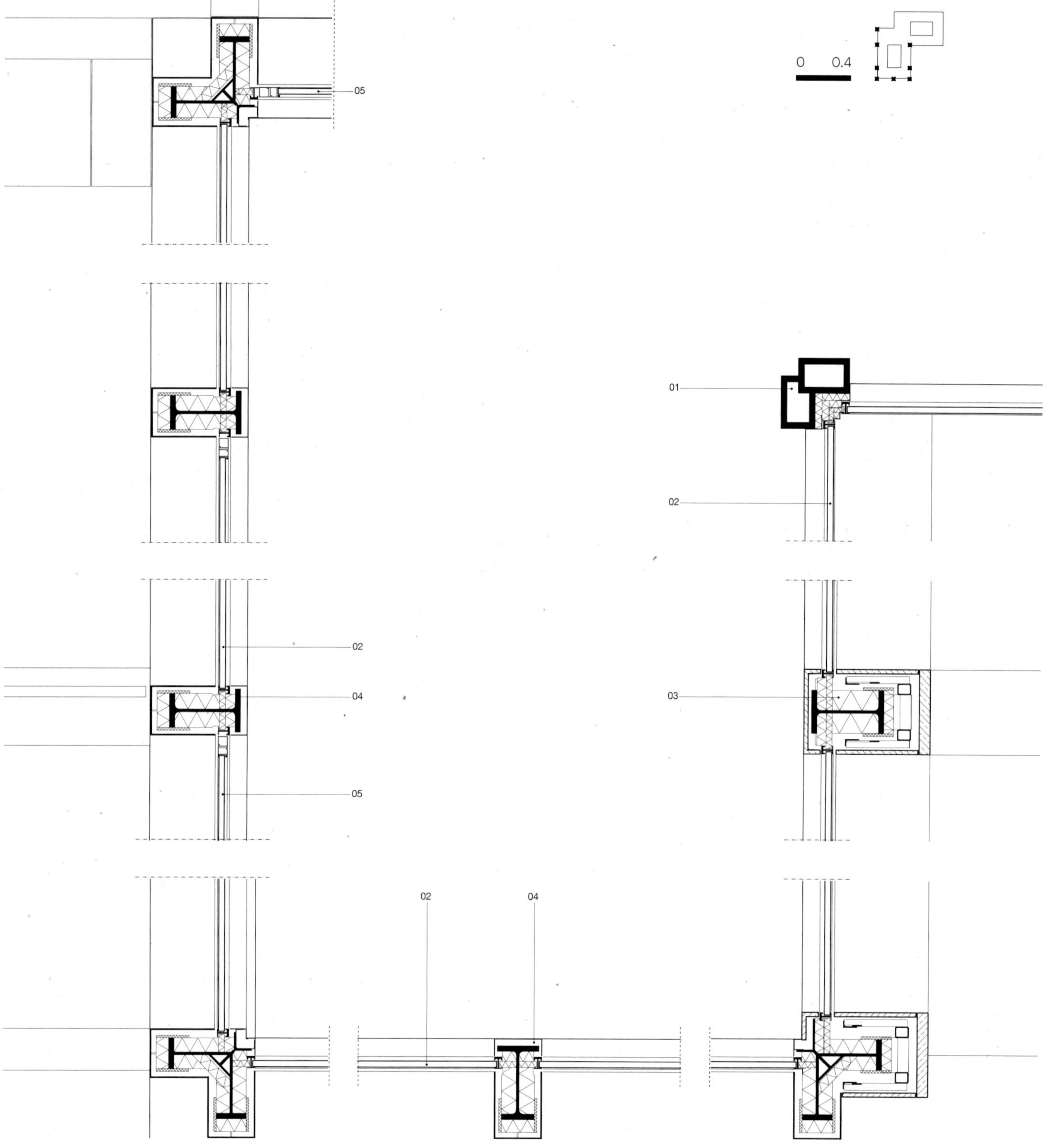

01 corner column
- main load bearing structure, compound profile, thickness: 45mm;
intumescent coating, colour: RAL 8022, glossiness 30%

02 facade
- steel curtain wall, rectangular box section transoms 140×80mm, vertically mounted to main load bearing structure
- glazing: 4.2.4 - 18A - 8.2.8, LTA: 67%, g-value: 0,34, reflectance: 13%

03 natural stone column (inside-to-outside)
- marble, polished: grain 220, hidden mounting with anchors, open joints 8mm to assist thermal pre-heating of column;
- main load bearing structure: HEM500, S460, intumescent coating on interior;
- insulated facade panel: steel sheet, galvanised, 0,7mm - rock wool 42mm - steel sheet, galvanised, 0,7mm;
- rock wool insulation, λ = 0,035 W/m.K, with aluminium foil facing, mechanical fixation; seams and exposed corners taped;
- steel support structure for fixation of natural stone elements, var. profiles;
- marble, polished: grain 220, hidden mounting with anchors, sealed joints (grout), grey

04 steel column (inside-to-outside)
- folded aluminium sheet element, 3mm, coating: RAL8022, glossiness 30%; hidden mounting with conversion brackets;
- main load bearing structure: HEM500, S460, intumescent coating on interior, exterior flange width reduced to 240mm;
- insulated facade panel: steel sheet, galvanised, 0,7mm - rockwool 42mm - steel sheet, galvanised, 0,7mm;
- rock wool insulation, λ = 0,035 W/m.K, with aluminium foil facing, mechanical fixation; seams and exposed corners taped;
- steel column cover element, 6mm, assembled, coating: finish layer: RAL8022, satin; hidden mounting to main load bearing structure along horizontal facade elements

05 emergency egress door
steel profile door, with glass infill
powder coating: RAL8022, glossiness 30%

horizontal connection in the form of a continuous metal profile was added between the columns. Apart from ensuring a continued rhythm of lines in the facade and a visual separation of floors from facades, these horizontals also compensate some of the stress on the columns from loads and wind. The stone cladding of the floor edges in combination with the floating effect strengthens the sense of the foyers being independent spaces.

ENGINEERING

Obviously this challenging design of meticulously co-ordinated parts had to be buildable. During the design stages, both the facade specialist and the manufacturer of the loadbearing steel skeleton stepped in early to work together with the design team and builder for the best construction solutions. Once the main technical details have been resolved, the sequence of assembly becomes an important issue, not only for the construction phase, but also for maintenance over the years. Up to the fifth floor, replacing windows will be done from the outside, which means the casings, flashings and stone cladding around the pilasters have to be removable. The columns were given anchor points for the construction hoist that would be necessary to handle the very heavy glass panes. The assembly (and later maintenance) sequence required careful assessment of tolerances and dimensions. By way of two mock-ups, all these aspects were tested and the problems encountered were solved early on. During construction, measurements were taken regularly to anticipate deviations, and special tools were used to limit assembly tolerances to just a few millimetres.

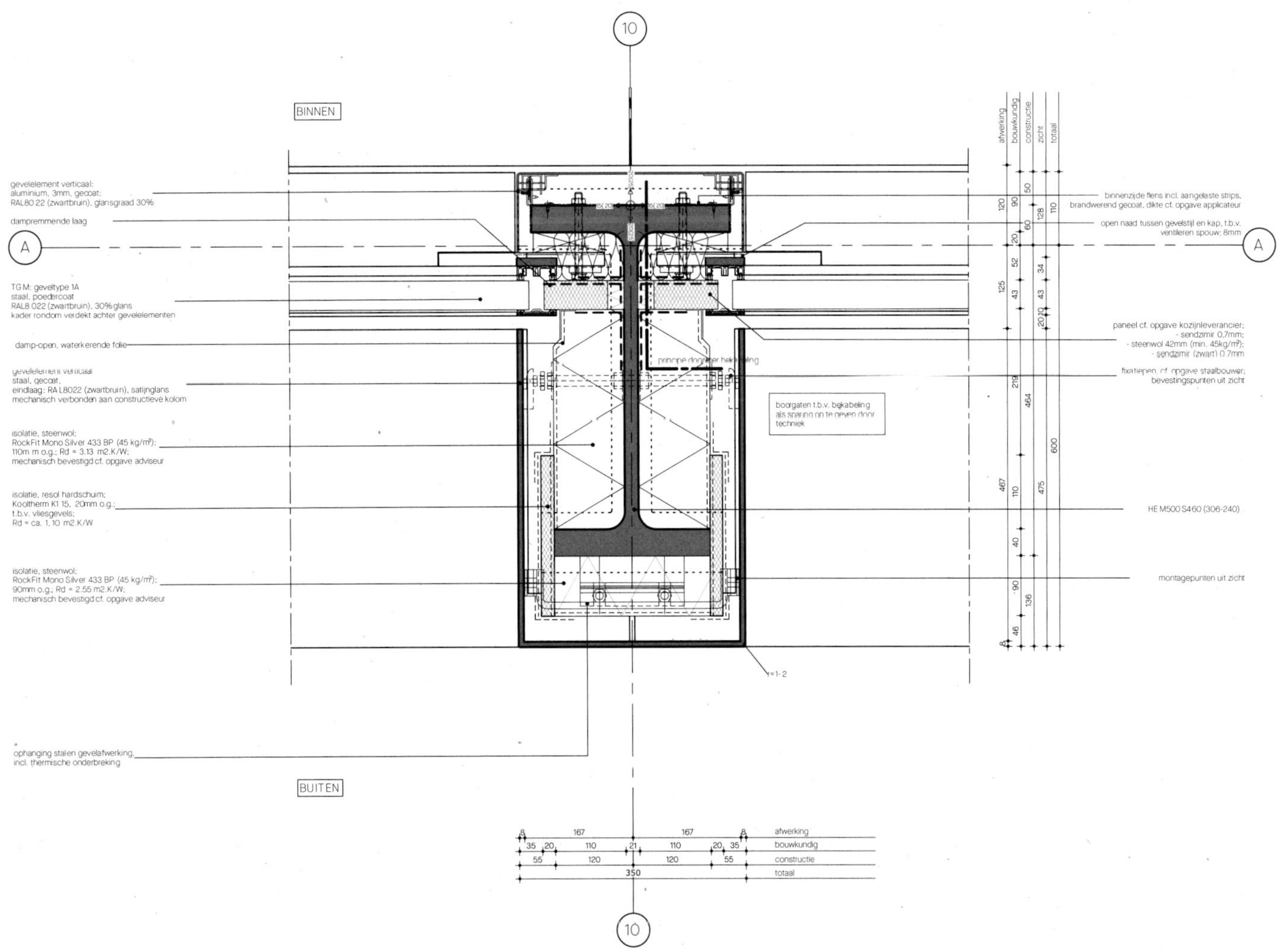

HORIZONTAL DETAIL OF STEEL FACADE COLUMN

Courtrooms

The specifications for the courtrooms were documented in detail: acoustic, visual and ergonomic comfort were essential requirements. This kind of dry and technical information only really came to life for the architects after attending some hearings, talking with judges and other users, and extensive testing and assessment sessions. In the words of one of the judges: 'This is a top-class sport, so we need a good pitch.'

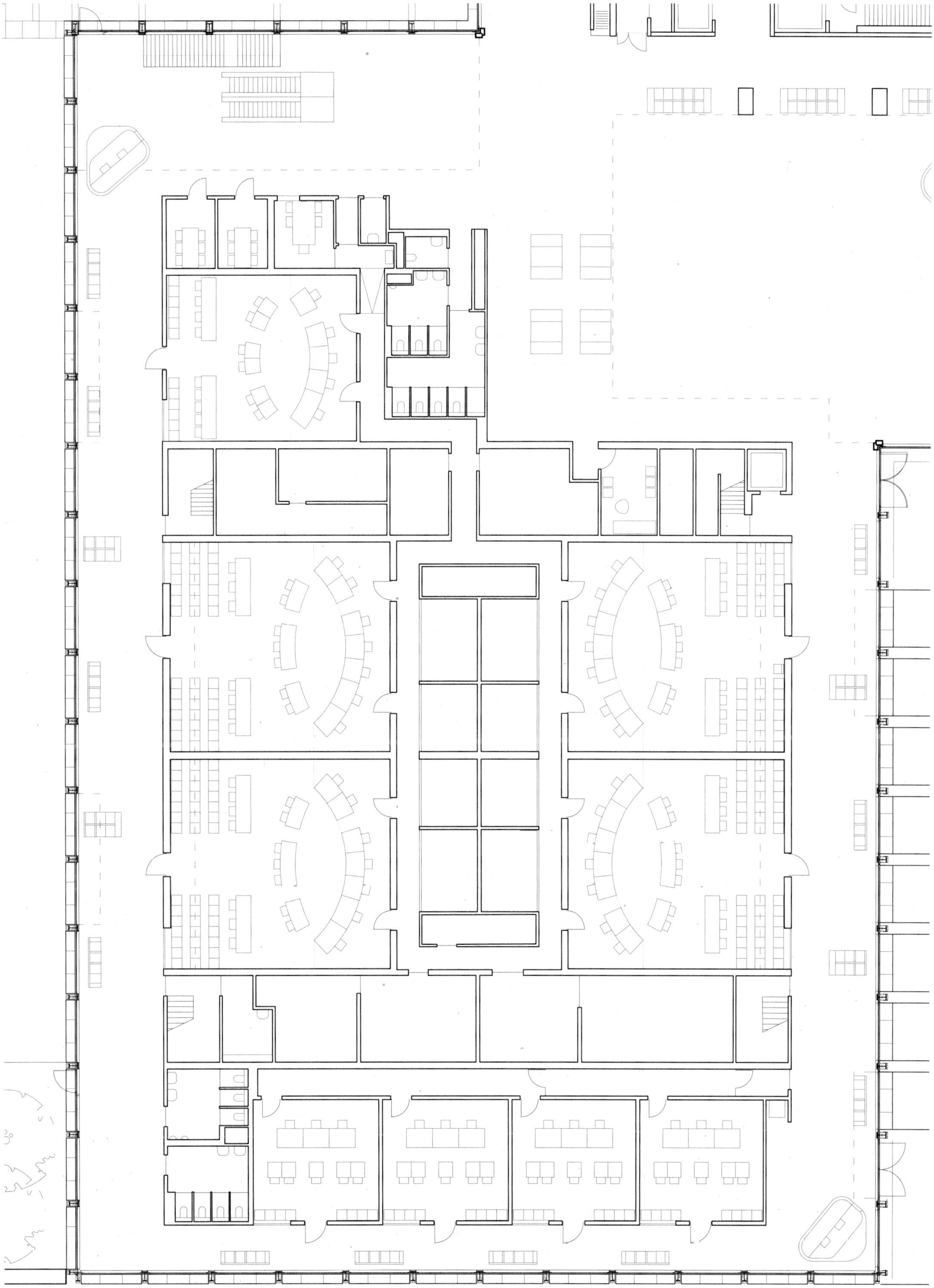

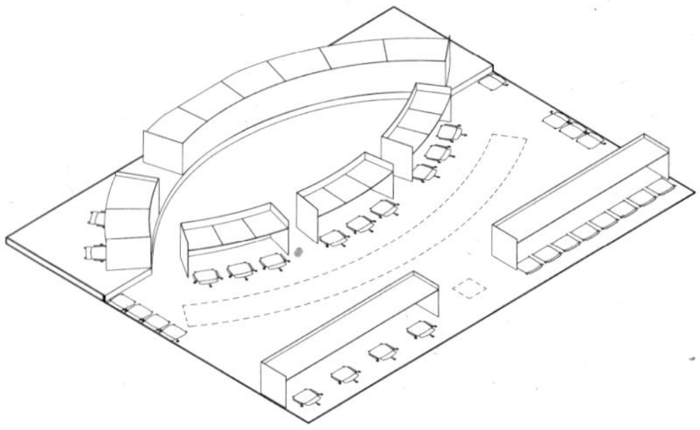

Extra-large courtroom

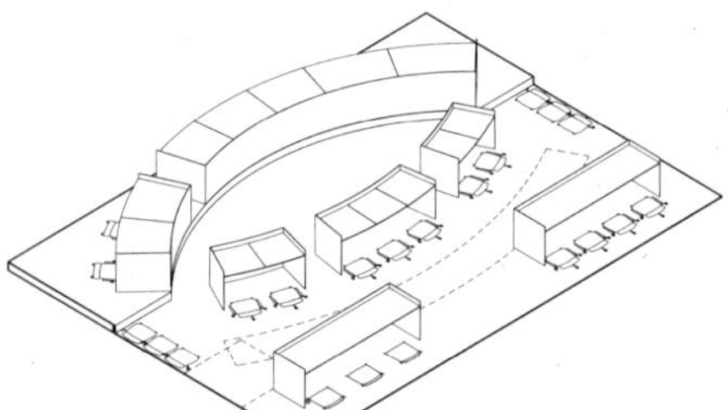

Large courtroom

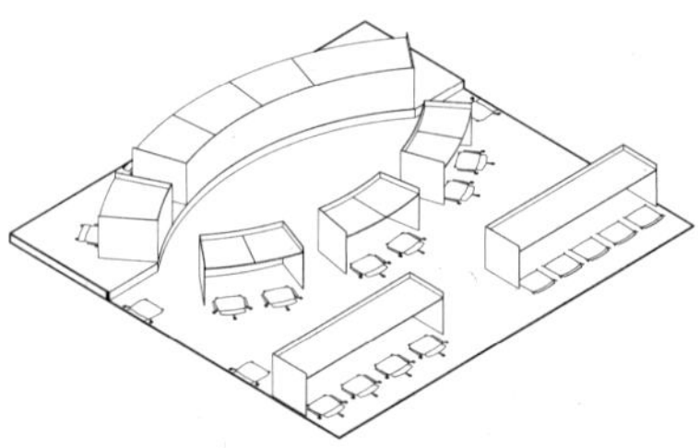

Regular courtroom with prosecution desk

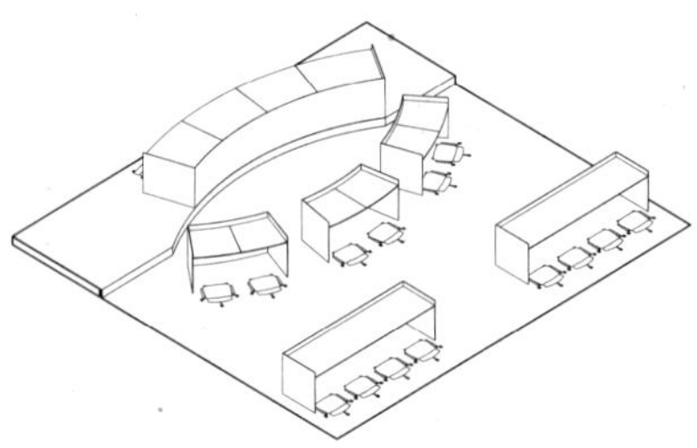

Regular courtroom without prosecution desk

COURTROOMS TYPES

TYPES

Apart from the desired openness, the courtrooms also needed to be designed based on their differing uses. Each type of courtroom has specific requirements with regard to dimensions and arrangement of furniture. For example, in the courtrooms for criminal cases, where the behaviour of some of those present can be unpredictable, extra space was reserved for security guards. These rooms have a direct and separate connection to the holding area downstairs. On the other hand, in the arraignment rooms everything is arranged around a large combined table. The larger courtrooms are furnished to accommodate a wide variety of arrangements, from hearings that attract extra press attention to large groups of suspects.

DAYLIGHT

Since a trial can last a whole day or even several days, the lighting conditions are an important consideration. Windows with views into a courtroom from the foyers (which have contact with daylight) would be unacceptable, but at the same time a view out from the judge's bench – to the weather outside, to gauge the time of day – is important. Since the judges face internal walls or public galleries, it was decided early on to provide each room with its own window feature that could bridge the foyers. These vertical glazed sections are frameless panes that transition from the foyers' marble walls without interruption. The dimensions of the glazing are in keeping with the walls, but what makes the transition so extraordinarily effective is the marbling on the glass. High resolution photographs were taken of the surfaces of four stone slabs prior to instalment. The images were variously rotated and mirrored to create 16 different prints. The architects assessed per location which print would be applied to which window, based on the most natural possible transition from adjacent marble slabs and also to avoid obvious print repetition.

The transparency of the prints was extensively tested in mock-ups: Is transparency the absence of printing ink, is it black or white, what ratio of opacity vs. transparency works best? Ultimately, the choice was to print a vertical gradient moving from more black ink below to more white ink above, and from opaque to translucent. This gives the people in the courtroom both privacy and some views. Finally, the mock-up also tested what the effect of changing light on either side of the glass would be on the transparency and reflection. The dimensions and resolution of the print demanded the utmost from the glass supplier and printer, so together they adapted their standard procedure templates to meet the demands. Along the edges of the windows, where the glass is glued to the frame, it was equally as important to conceal the seam with a fluid continuation of print. Behind the printed glass is the actual framing, which guarantees fire protection and good acoustics. The frames for the glazing in the large courtrooms on the ground floor are so large that they required greater tolerances in case of fire (when glass expands due to heat). Of course, this translates into wider seams with the adjoining stone walls, and to avoid this becoming too apparent, extra strips were added to the glass frames so that the pieces of 'marbled glass' would bond well enough in their sockets while still maintaining flow in the pattern.

All the windows facing the outdoors have interior structures to house blinds where necessary. These may be needed for a variety of reasons: in some cases to shield from being seen by the outside world, but naturally also for shade or darkness. A low sun must not be allowed to shine annoyingly into the eyes, and it should be possible to create sufficient darkness for showing digital images. Wherever possible these functions were combined in a single

blind so that the visual impact does not become obtrusive. When fully opened, the blinds disappear into the wall above; at the press of a button, a court clerk can lower them in total silence.

ARTIFICIAL LIGHT

Artificial lighting is subject to just as many technical and aesthetic requirements as daylight. The basic infrastructure consists of spotlights in the ceiling combined with an accent in the recessed ventilation line along the edge of the ceiling. While the spotlights provide the necessary level of lighting for work and reading, it is the accent line that gives the room a special ambience. The pendant lights above the judges' benches resulted from experience: judges found that the high ceiling spotlights in other courtrooms sometimes caused annoying reflections on their computer screens (often laid flat). The design team initially investigated whether this problem could be resolved by very wide spotlights with a matte covering, but the ideal setup for this was not in keeping with the broader ceiling plan. Further laboratory tests ultimately showed that lowering the light by means of pendant fixtures has a positive effect on legibility.

FLOORS

The floor of every courtroom is fitted with circular outlet boxes for audio-visual facilities and laptops, and the power supply runs under the floor in conduits. These conduits still have ample room in them for future wiring so the floor need not be broken up for future renovation. Under the judges' benches there are so many cables and pipes that placing a raised floor (also called computer floor) was better than laying a fixed floor.

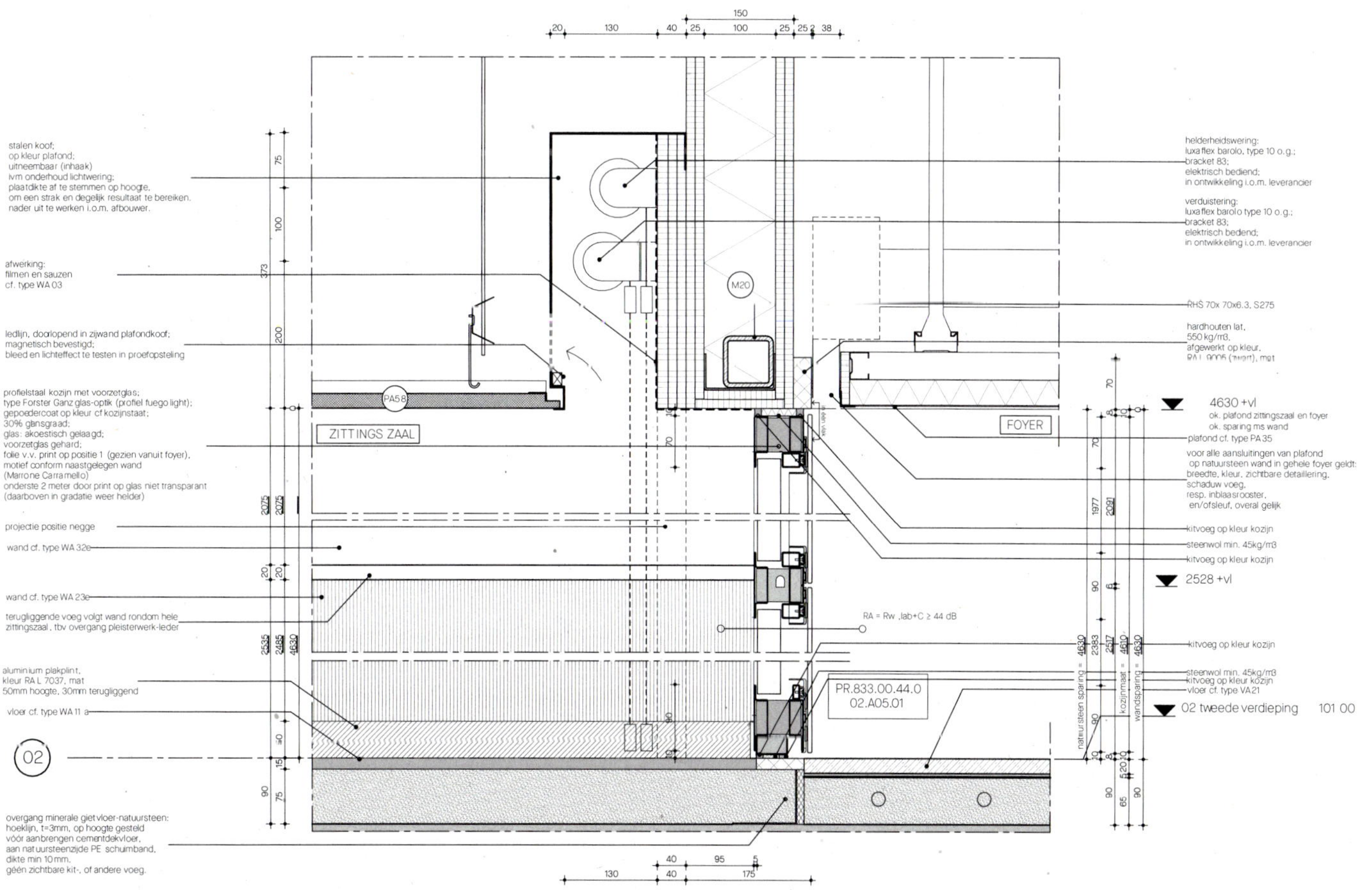

VERTICAL DETAIL OF COURTROOM WINDOW WITH MARBLE PRINT

The conduits were positioned in the floor at sufficient distances from each other so that the poured concrete had enough space to form properly and avoid future cracking. The underfloor outlet boxes are positioned so as to disappear under the tables, which means no unsightly cables and sockets to disturb the calmness of the courtrooms, and their finishing covers are in the same polished concrete as the rest of the floor. Since a concrete floor is poured before the outlets can be inserted, achieving a colour match in the covers was no small challenge. It was essential to record the exact ratio and brand of ingredients used for each floor in order to replicate these for each courtroom.

The floors also contain installations for the hearing impaired. A conductor loop was placed in the concrete underfloor when poured, with the density of the wires decreasing further away from the centre of the room. The best reception is therefore in the centre of the courtroom; as you move outwards, the number of wires and the quality of reception decrease. This prevents eavesdropping or inadvertently picking up conversations outside the courtroom.

WALLS

When it comes to acoustics, it is very important for all parties to hear both unamplified and amplified sounds effectively under all circumstances. Every possible surface of the courtroom was therefore assessed for its acoustic properties and requirements. The reverberation time, speech intelligibility and sound frequencies for various materials were determined by means of simulations during the design phase. And during construction, the simulations were tested and substantiated in a test room. As a result, almost every surface achieved an attenuating and/or dissipating effect. An important point of attention was preventing 'flutter', sound waves bouncing back and forth between the courtroom walls. This consideration influenced the choice for a soft wall finish that would both absorb and disperse noise, and also give the room a warm feeling. Vertically ribbed leather panels reaching 2.60 metres high embrace the room and thus create optimal circumstances for hearing. At first the leather was simply attached to a backing in a wave pattern, but once applied to the wall it became clear that this was not a durable implementation, and certainly not up to the standards of a courtroom – it would dent or loosen or even rip over time.

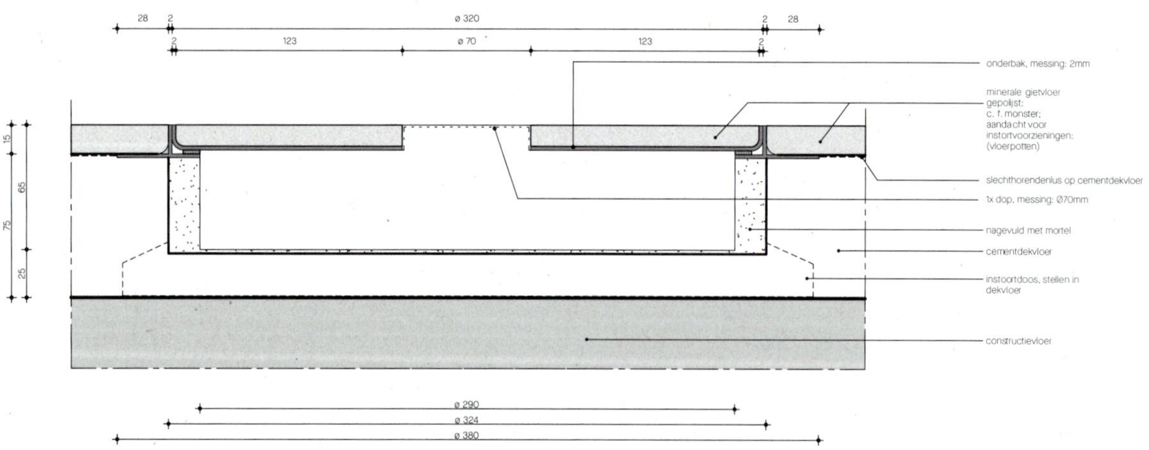

VERTICAL DETAIL OF FLOOR OUTLET POINT

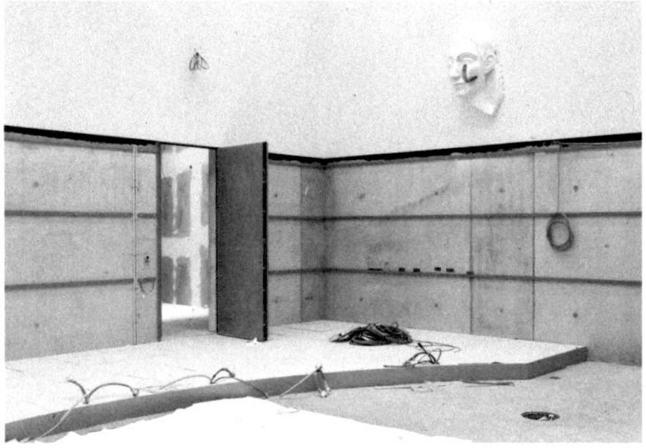

Many incarnations later, the design team arrived at a softer, pseudo-suede material glued onto milled half-cylinder wooden strips. The vertical ribbing was composed to form a neutral background for the courtroom, but it was also necessary to avoid a pronounced moiré effect, which is disorientating for some. The panels are further detailed with round corners, ribbing that flattens out around electrical service points, and even the door spigots are integrated in the ribbing to fall flush with the doors. The individual panels can be removed for easy maintenance or replacement, so the upper backside of the panels was precisely the right spot to run circular cable ducts for any future AV technical changes. Above the leather panels, the walls have sound insulation behind a layer of sprayed plaster. This is also the zone allocated for art.

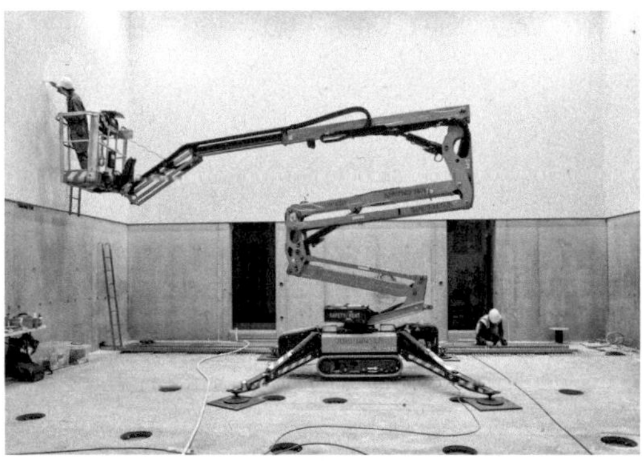

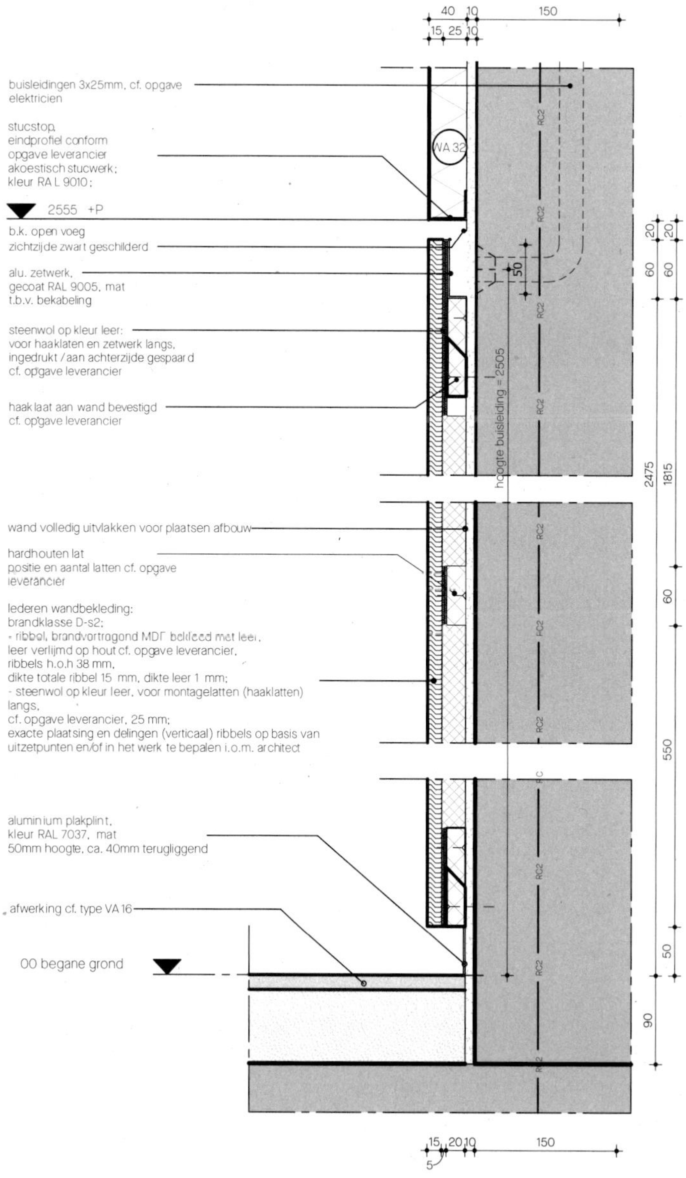

VERTICAL DETAIL OF LEATHER WALL PANELING

GALLERIES

In the seven large courtrooms on the ground floor the public galleries are balconies (not unlike theatre balconies) that are accessed from the foyers on the floor above. This reduces the intrusiveness of observers entering the courtroom.

It was a precondition for the galleries to be provided with full views of the room. A visitor should be able to follow the proceedings without any technical aids or amplifiers. Since the large courtrooms – though not the one extra-large courtroom – are all quite shallow, studies were conducted early in the design process to determine the optimal lines of sight. Narrow steps between the seating allowed a good overview for all those seated of the judge's bench, the litigants and defendants, and the information screens.

Glass screens safely separate the gallery from the ground floor of the courtroom and contribute to acoustic containment. The screens were designed without any visible vertical lines. At the top, the glass panes are clamped into steel racks that also serve as support for the ventilation ducts, which are wrapped for acoustic resistance.

The finishes and furnishings of the galleries are low-maintenance and vandal-proof. Loose furniture was ruled out on account of the potential for aggression. Each row of seats has a place at one end for a wheelchair, which can also be used as a waiting area for a court security officer.

FURNITURE

In addition to high ergonomic standards, the furniture had to meet the high demands of flexibility and usability. Because the setup of a courtroom sometimes needs to change, the designers researched the greatest common denominators for the tables at which litigants sit, for this was to be the most basic building block for the furnishings. Many aspects were considered, such as a minimum table surface area for placing a laptop and papers, logical positions for the electrical fittings (for AV equipment and microphones), sufficient space between the table legs, and the remaining space to move around in the room. There had to be enough space for the armed guards to be able to intervene quickly in case of a disturbance. All these prerequisites ultimately shaped the final module: a slightly curved single table. Two variants were then developed on the basis of the module: one standard without technical additions, for defendants, witnesses and others present, and one for lawyers, equipped with AV connections and adjustable in height. The tables can be linked together and are equipped with magnets to attach end panels and side panels. This flexibility allows tables to be moved also from room to room, so there is never a need to keep rooms full of furniture. The contract demanded that there be a protocol for setting up a courtroom for use. For example, how quickly and how often a layout can be changed, what the deadline is for requesting a change, and how many layout variants can be placed in the building at the same time. All this determined the variety and size of the furniture, and provided a guide for determining the best locations for storage areas throughout the building.

The choice of chairs for the various parties – the judges, those at the counsel tables, the public – was made in close consultation with Courthouse staff. An initial selection of three options for each type of chair was put on display during a feedback session in the old courthouse. Everyone could indicate their favourite. The focus was not on pretty or ugly, but on objective characteristics such as dimensions, manageability and flexibility. The opinions of information desk staff and security guards weighed heavily since in practice they handle the furniture the most. Chairs with sharp corners were rejected, as were those with soft fabric upholstery. The former because, in the worst case, they could be used as a weapon, and the latter because, paradoxically, they do not fare well in rough daily use.

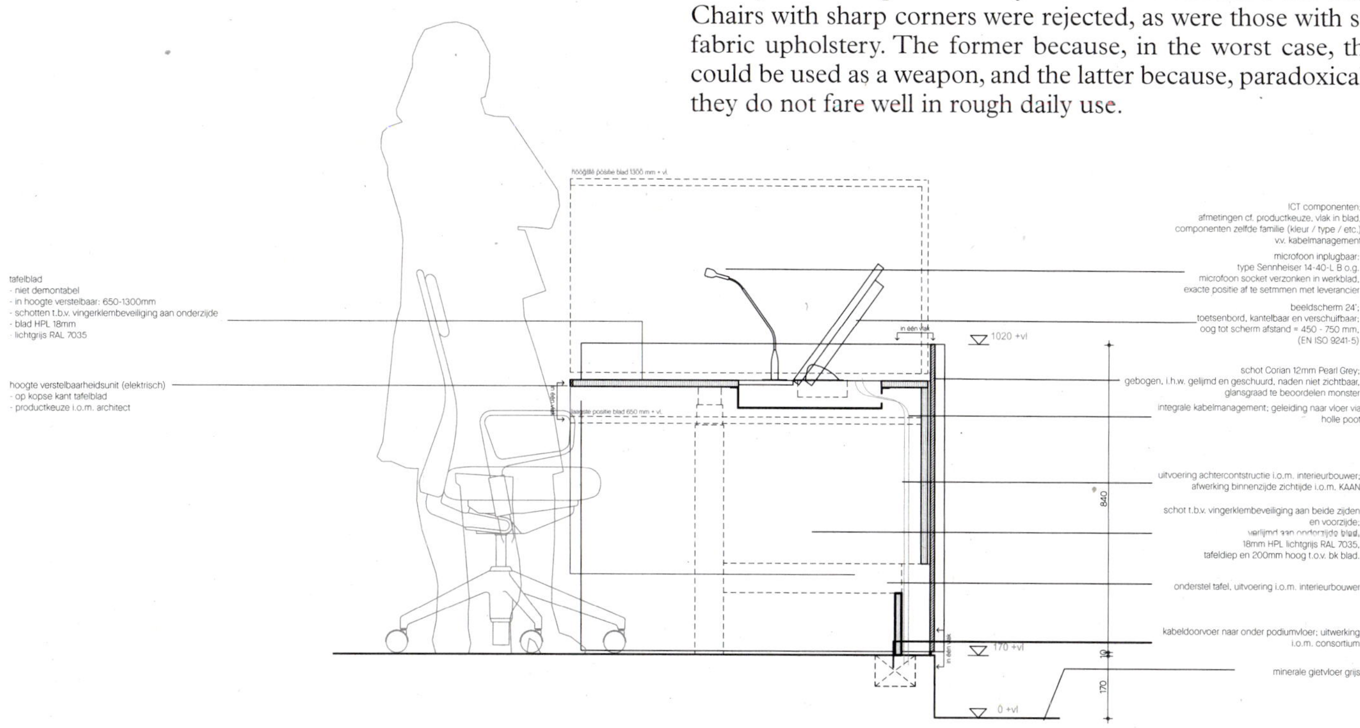

VERTICAL DETAIL OF MAGISTRATES TABLE

Ramps and Gardens

The west side of the building provides access via ramps to the underground holding area for detainees and the underground parking garage. For security reasons, the courthouse has separate entrances and exits for the transportation of detainees, and requires a minimum distance between these routes as well as a prescribed minimum speed. In addition, the parking garage for staff and visitors also required a separate ramp to take them from street level down to the second underground level.

BASEMENT

The groundwater level at this site was a decisive factor for the depth of the basement; around the courthouse the water table is about 1 metre below street level. Going underground, which was always going to be necessary, meant coming up with a solution for draining the site during construction and building a waterproof wall. A wet excavation pit and underwater concrete were ruled out because these would lengthen the construction time. This decision dictated the deepest possible depth for the lowest building layer. Any deeper than 7.5 metres and there was no guarantee that the pumping mills would keep the basement walls dry. The high ceiling of the first basement level was dictated by the height of the detainee transport buses. The space left over for a level below this would have been insufficient, were it not for the fact that – for aesthetic, urban planning and security reasons – the building was already planned on a base of 90 centimetres. This extra height provided exactly enough room to realize both parking levels in the basement and also gave more space to the sunken garden and views onto it from the inside.

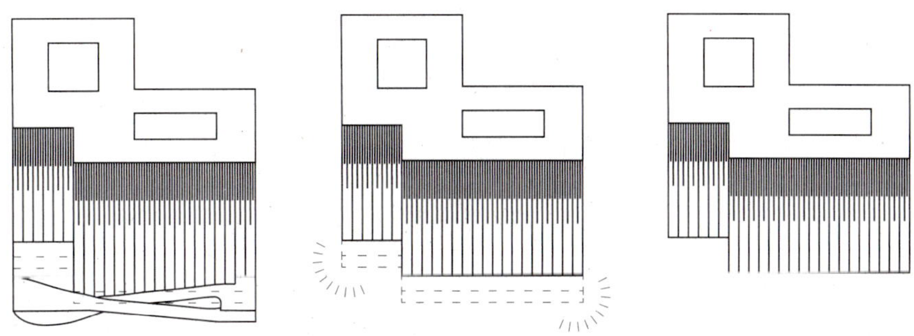

RAMPS

The best routes to both basement levels were worked out in consultation with parking experts, first in two-dimensional drawings, then in a three-dimensional computer model. The staff parking entrance required considerably more creativity than the entrance for the Security, Surveillance & Transport (SS&T) vehicles, despite the big bus sizes, which essentially required no more than a straightforward ramp. NEN2443 is the Dutch building norm that sets out design conditions for parking garages: the length of a ramp is linked to the maximum permitted gradient (the longer the ramp, the less steep it may be), in order to provide the most comfortable and safest driving experience possible. For the courthouse, this translated into a ramp of almost 75 metres in length, to which a waiting area, height transitions and exit length would have to be added. That's almost twice the size of the available building plot. By dividing the ramp into shorter sections, each section being permitted to have a steeper gradient, plus creating short near-horizontal sections between them, it was finally possible to bridge the difference in height as comfortably as possible. The decision to have both ramps hook into each other works wonders. Extra space for waiting cars at the staff entrance was created by bridging over the SS&T entrance. After the waiting area, cars make a 90 degree turn to the left where the ramp leads down to the garage, in the opposite direction to the SS&T ramp – though, importantly, users are unable to see each other. A second 90 degree turn to the right leads down to the second underground parking level. The additional length in the horizontal sections optimizes the gradient. The interweaving of the ramps is quite sculptural, especially when viewed from above.

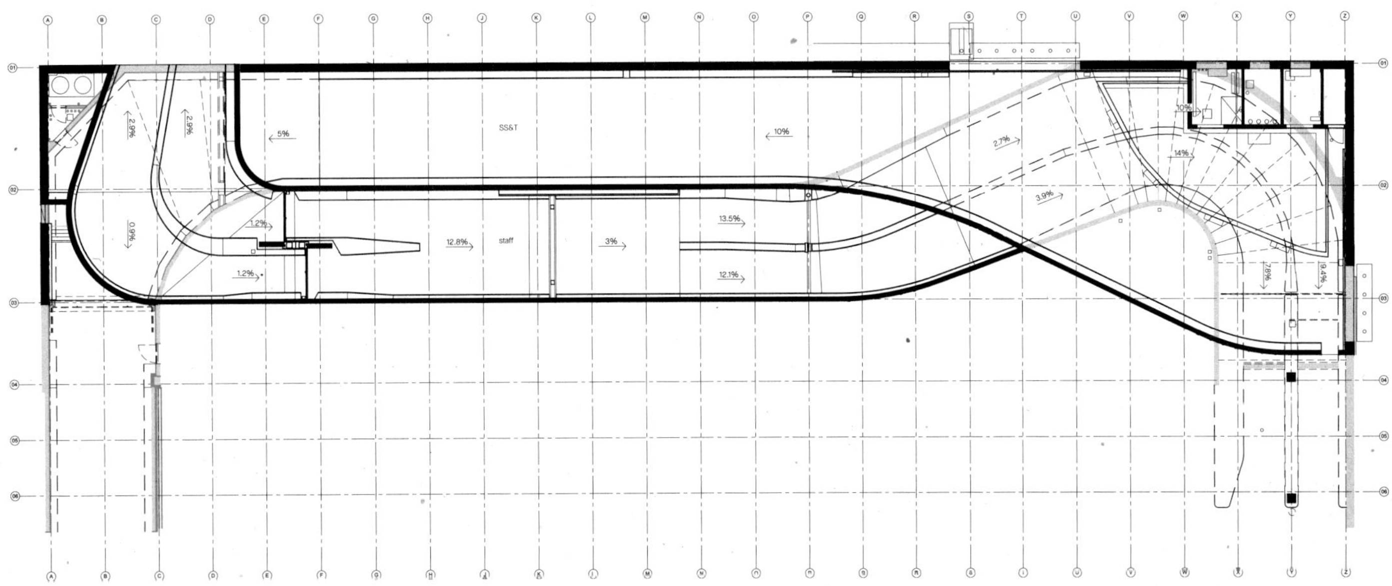

PLAN OF RAMPS FOR SS&T AND STAFF

GARDEN WALLS

The aesthetics of the necessary ramps and walls plays just as important a role in the design as integrating the functional and programme requirements. The client stipulated that the separate ramp routes should be as invisible as possible: invisible to each other, to the outside world and to the interior. The ramps are therefore separated by walls. The walls are high enough to prevent people seeing in from street level, but low enough at street level (an average human height) to feel comfortable. Also from inside the building, the walled stone-clad enclosure feels completely open to the sky. The walls outside of the direct view of the public in the foyers were not clad in stone, but the quality of the concrete still had to meet high aesthetic demands. In order to make it blend with the stone cladding as much as possible, the divisions in the concrete formwork and the positions of the centre pins were coordinated to have the same dimensions as the stone slabs, and this was detailed in drawings as well. The colour of the concrete was determined after a number of test pours, after which the precise composition of the mix was constantly monitored during the various pours. The architects were present when the formwork was removed to immediately check for any imperfections and, in consultation with site supervisors, determine any corrective measures to be taken. Below ground level, the aesthetic requirements for the concrete were less stringent. Waterproofing the concrete was the priority here. Nevertheless, the colours were still successfully matched.

The architects paid extra attention to the transitions between the various materials and substrates. The concrete wall tapers where it transitions to stone slabs, so there is no difference in planes. The width of the transition seam here is the same as that between the stone slabs. The stone slabs were cut to size on site to achieve the tightest fit. And finally, above the ramp for staff/visitor cars there is no concrete substrate, a suspended steel structure supports the stone.

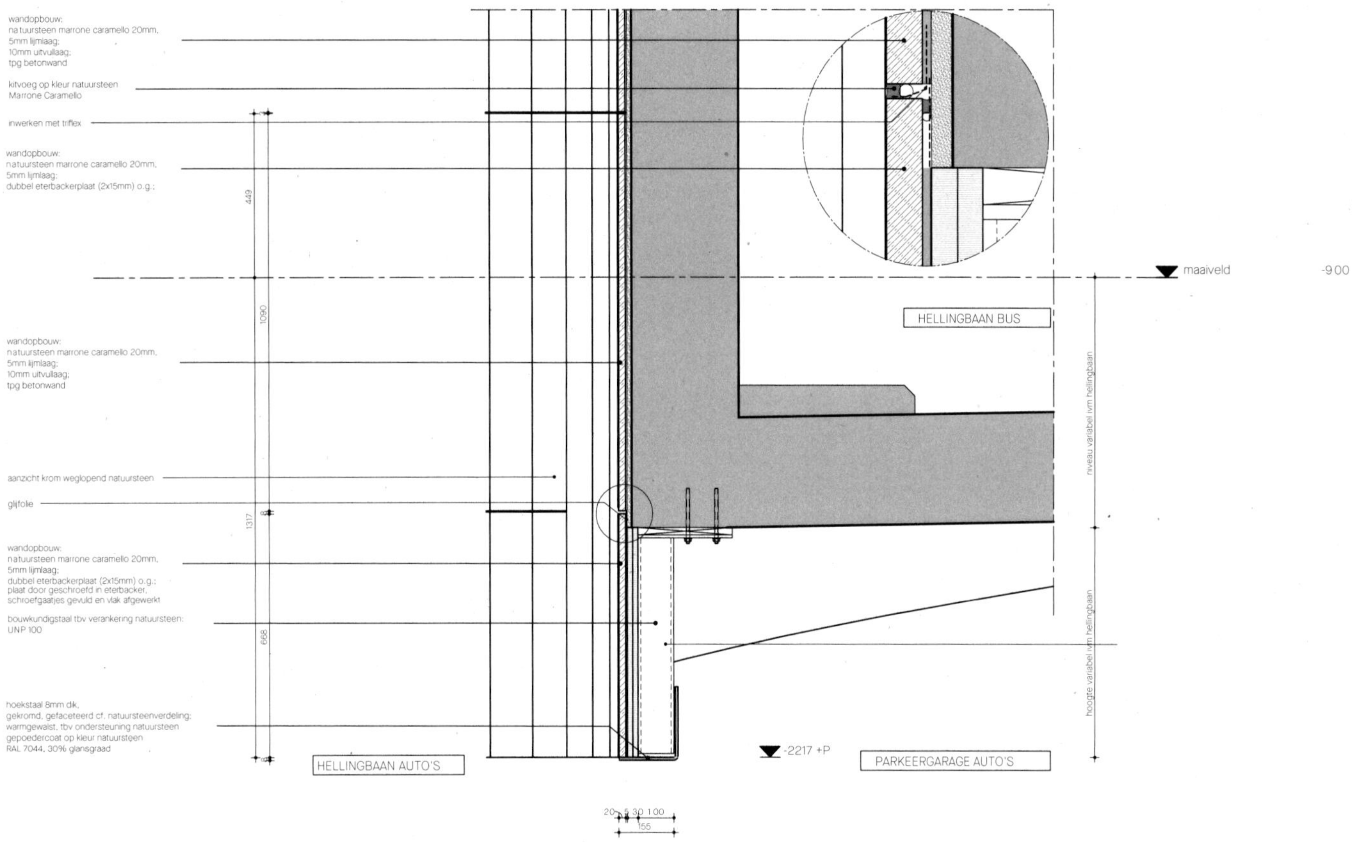

VERTICAL DETAIL OF RAMP AND NATURAL STONE CLADDING

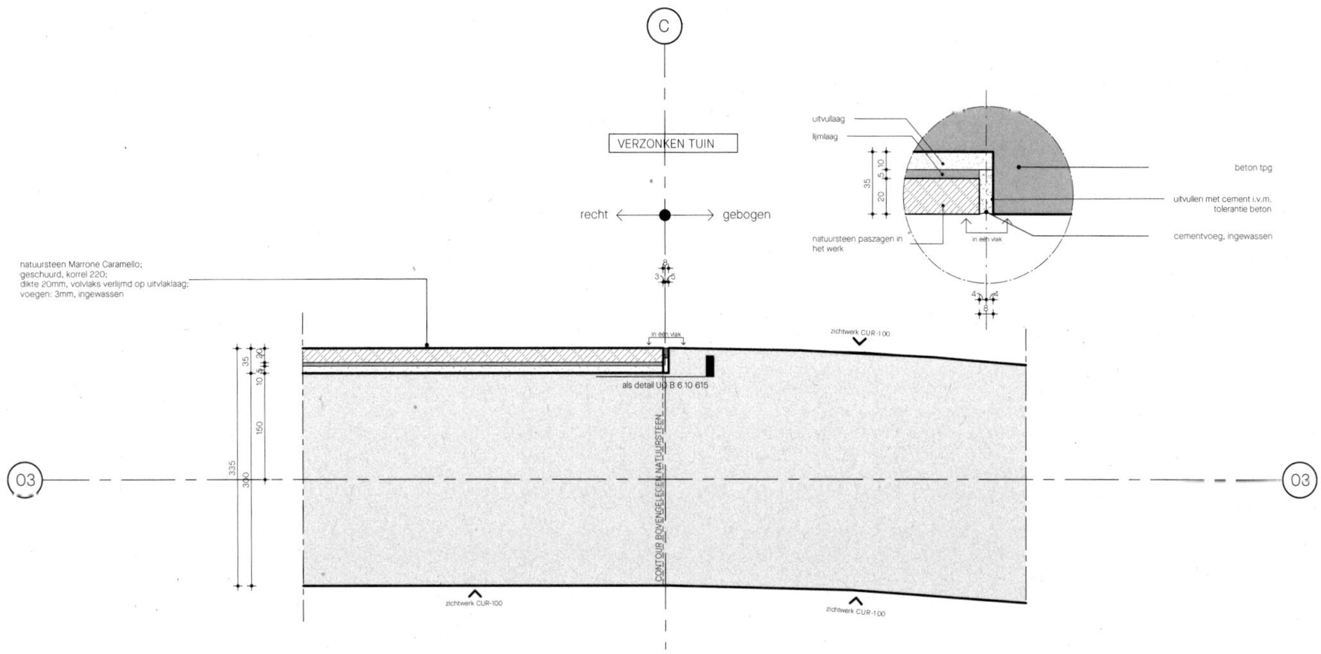

HORIZONTAL DETAIL OF THE TRANSITION POINT BETWEEN
EXPOSED CONCRETE WALL AND NATURAL STONE CLADDING

HORTUS CONCLUSUS

The enclosed garden, a *hortus conclusus*, in the north-west corner of the site is also part of the sculpture of the access ramps. This garden is out of sight for pedestrians, apart from the greenery that protrudes above the wall. On the inside it is in full view, though not accessible to visitors. The basic layout consists of a square on the north side plus steps down to a long sunken garden on the west side. Sightlines play a crucial role in the landscape design, as did adding elements that would align with the robust architecture of the building. The undulating ramp walls that separate the different routes from each other were an inspiration for the landscaping of undulating bands, as wide as the walls and clad with the same stone. A few of these bands gradually descend to the garden level (the level of the base of the building) to merge with the ground level (the street level). The stone bands also separate green areas from semi-paved areas with small (12-18 millimetre) white gravel as ground cover. All the greys of the garden are in keeping with the architectural palette, creating a soft, harmonious whole. The plant beds feature mainly plants with long leaves, interspersed with clusters of flowering plants (allium, anemone) that brightening the garden. Several multi-stemmed and single-stemmed Gleditsia trees, with their elegant cast shadows, form the ideal background for the spatial sequence from the forecourt, via the central hall, to the enclosed garden. The Gleditsia is an open, airy tree that has also been planted elsewhere in the neighbourhood and six generous specimens now also populate the courthouse's front square.

The enclosed garden continues into the sunken garden along the west facade on Level -1 and is connected by a staircase. This staircase follows the diagonal line of the ramps. The sunken garden is dressed in the same gravel as that used in the enclosed garden and features a few climbing plants against the descending ramp wall. The combination of the grey marble cladding and the changing colours of the leaves provide an attractive view throughout the year.

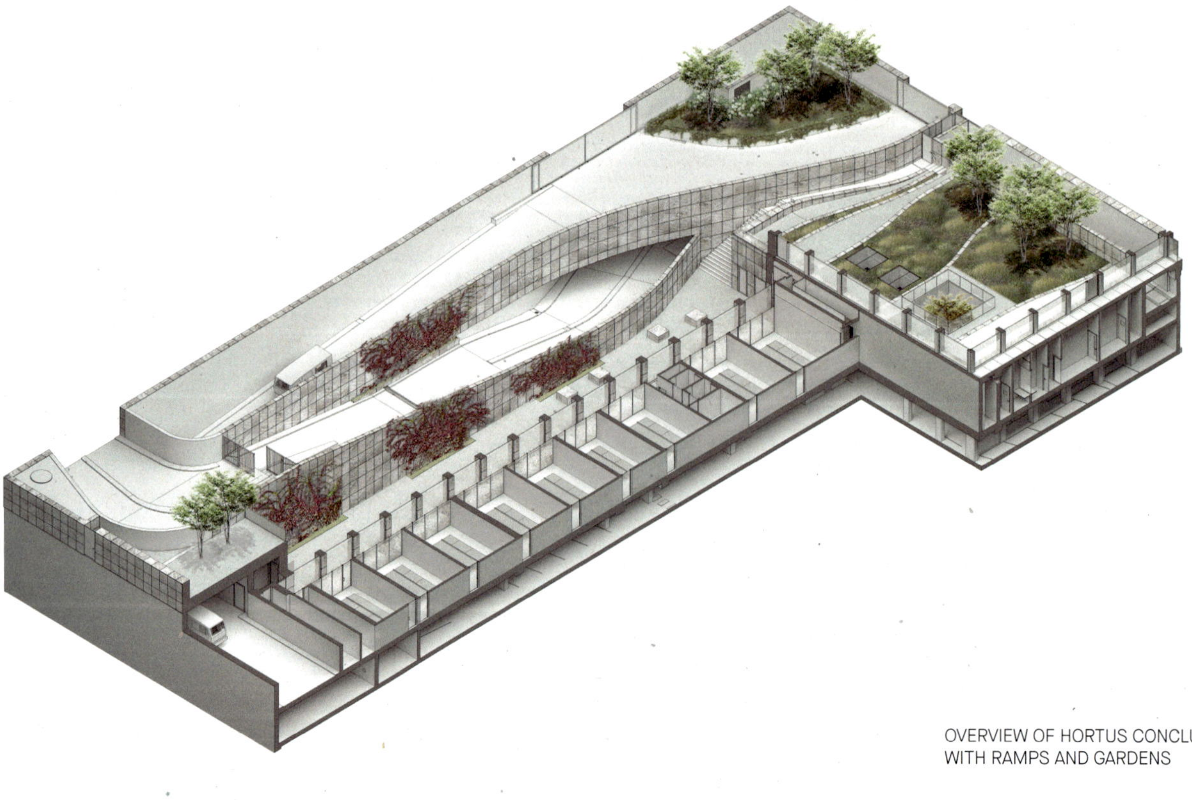

OVERVIEW OF HORTUS CONCLUSUS
WITH RAMPS AND GARDENS

V.
Art Makes Connections

In the Netherlands, all buildings funded by the state have a budget for fine art in the building. That this should also apply to a courthouse is self-evident. After all, a courthouse is not a sterile, isolated world of law, but a real-world place where daily life happens. Art is capable of not only highlighting the connection between life (or society) and the law, it can also stimulate it, as the observations in this chapter make clear.

In the case of the Amsterdam Courthouse, there are other reasons that art would naturally be included in furnishing the building. Perhaps the first and foremost reason is the fact of the Courthouse's own art collection, an impressive one built up over many years. While art is simply interesting in its own right, the Courthouse collection has also been driven by functional considerations. The visual arts bring a worthy dimension to both a working environment and the public space of a building, for art can be thought-provoking and also put things into perspective. Finally, the nature of the new building itself, in its spatiality and orientation to serving society, extends a very welcoming hand to art.

HANS DEN HARTOG JAGER

Lady Justice, Let Your Blindfold Fall

FEMMY OTTEN, *UNTITLED*

I.

If there is one thing that can be said about the art in the new Amsterdam Courthouse, it's that it's got a lot of eyes on it. It starts with Nicole Eisenman's monumental sculpture on the square. This is a figure of a man, a boy or a girl who has just gathered three little things in their hand and is examining them intensely: an owl, an arrow and an acorn. Then there's the eyes *in* the art: the 13 works by Dutch artist Femmy Otten for the seven large courtrooms have a lot of eyes in them, sometimes prominently, sometimes inconspicuously. The most striking piece is undoubtedly the gold medallion in the Amstel Courtroom that bulges out of the wall and is crowned by a piercing eye – a powerful representation of the divine all-seeing eye.

And have you noticed that the judges' benches and counsel tables in the courtrooms form the shape of an eye?

It's almost a provocation, all those eyes. The most traditional symbol for justice is the figure of Lady Justice, adorned with a sword and scales – and of course, a blindfold. Justitia's blindness stands for the impartial perspective of the law, but may also suggest that she does not need the world around her to come to a verdict. This idea has certainly changed over the past few decades. Judges, lawyers, maybe even suspects, are increasingly aware that the law does not take place in a timeless vacuum, but that every legal proceeding has its roots in an event that took place in real life, in real society and that, moreover, every verdict contributes to a new ordering of that society. Not a blindfold, then, but an open outlook.

This change is well-illustrated by all the art in the new courthouse. *Look*, the art seems to say, *the law is not anonymous here, we are not blindfolded, we see you and we speak from a position of openness, interest, involvement in the world and humanity.* Yet at the same time, they also show that this view, this vision, cannot afford to become personal or subjective. The law must not discriminate. This tension is surely one of the most fascinating aspects of contemporary law: that, despite an ever-changing society that is becoming increasingly complex, it continues to seek the values that bind us humans together. Through law we continue to search for the foundations of what it means to live together. And the law strives for truth, while also understanding that there is not a single truth.

Bridging this tension between the individual and the truth is precisely what comes to the fore in the courthouse works of Eisenman, Otten and Wine. In their work, all three artists explicitly seek to connect everyday life with universal, timeless ideas. They do so primarily by using two artistic instruments of connection: symbols and allegories (which the law also likes to do, see Lady Justice). In turn, symbols and allegories rely on two 'techniques' to communicate their message: isolation and distortion. These elements, these techniques, recur in almost all the works of art in the new courthouse. They are almost a catalogue on how to make connections.

How this works is beautifully illustrated in the four sculptures by Jesse Wine, presented on concrete pedestals in the sunken garden along the west side of the building. Here are four 'representations' in stone: two fingers crossed, a pile of half-deflated balls, an abstracted human vertebra and an 'absent' poem. At first glance, there seems to be no connection between them, but of course there is. The theme is connection itself: 'Know that you aren't alone,' as poet Vikram Seth wrote. His poem is printed on the windows of the two floors opposite the 'empty' pedestal – it is left up to the viewer to make the connection between the poem and the emptiness.

The same concept of connection is present in Wine's other sculptures. The two fingers form the symbol of 'luck' and the sundial is a sign of mankind's bond with light and nature. The three balls represent the three judges who must jointly reach a verdict, and thus seek unity in diversity. The vertebra stands for individual strength, but simultaneously also for the fact that a single vertebra can only mean something as part of a greater whole. Wine perfectly illustrates the power of symbols: by creating ordinary objects from unexpected materials and by removing them from their ordinary context (the human body, a game), you are prompted to think about their meaning. You connect with the art, and in turn, the art confronts or connects you with eternal concepts like luck and nature – and connection.

Femmy Otten's works in the seven large courtrooms take this a step further. Otten is known for work that attempts to unite eternal concepts such as time, love, healing and power. She seamlessly combines ideas that are unmistakably contemporary and personal with shapes and images almost directly extracted from other eras and cultures: early Renaissance paintings from Italy, for example, the shapes and images of the ancient Greeks, or art from the legendary Cambodian temple complex of Angkor Wat. And let's not forget Surrealism, which, not insignificantly, was a movement that aimed to express universality through the eternal and the subconscious. For Otten, this subtle link to Surrealism means above all the freedom to create her own world, unhindered by time and place. Incredibly, this world is also very much of today, yet still manages to connect the viewer to eternity – however incongruous this may seem at times.

All these diverse elements make Otten's world vast, and that's the beauty of it. Some of her works seem very clear in their meaning, such as the large paintings of the sea and sky that hang opposite each other at different heights in the Amsterdam Courtroom. Others are more poetic and surprising, such as the perfectly round rainbow in the IJ Courtroom, which is not only a beautiful symbol of unity, but also a beacon of light – she painted the rainbow in such intense colours that they seem to glow. At the same time, Otten's art communicates something subtle about what happens in courtrooms. The search for truth, for instance, is reflected in a number of *trompe-l'oeils*, such as the seemingly insignificant piece of wood that floats on the wall of the Herengracht Courtroom and the 'flying carpet' in the Keizersgracht Courtroom. It's as if Otten is subtly

JESSE WINE, *UNTITLED*

JESSE WINE, *UNTITLED*

FEMMY OTTEN, *UNTITLED*

FEMMY OTTEN, *UNTITLED*

FEMMY OTTEN, *UNTITLED*

but assertively pointing out that in order to find the truth, you sometimes have to look a little further than first impressions – and the *trompe-l'oeil* (deceive the eye) technique gives it all the more punch.

And then there are all those eyes in Otten's work. Sometimes they are surrealist/absurd, like the fantastical sculpture in the Singel Courtroom of an almost alien clump of matter with senses, or the romantic/poetic flying bird-carpet that throws us for a loop but also features a very small golden eye in the middle. The fact that Otten placed the works on opposite walls in all the courtrooms creates an excellent effect: they communicate with each other and this makes us want to be part of the conversation. In this regard, the judges, lawyers and defendants become the connecting factors – thus emphasizing once again that the law represents primarily the human need for connection.

It is for this exact same reason that Nicole Eisenman's giant sculpture on the square is so good. Eisenman first garnered attention with her stylized paintings of crowded scenes (people in parks, at the table, in bed) full of slightly absurd, chaotic events and full of references to pop culture and art history. In these works she demonstrates how seemingly unconnected elements can still be put together to create a harmonious world. And this is precisely what she does in her sculpture for the courthouse. It starts with the materials used. While classic outdoor statues are usually made of a single material, like bronze, Eisenman's figure is made of three different materials: bronze for the upper body, aluminium for the trousers, and composite marble for the boots. Then there is the aspect of time. While most sculptors aim to express timelessness by avoiding explicit references to fashion or trends, Eisenman does the opposite: everyone will recognize the Adidas stripes on the trousers and the Timberland brand of the boots. This makes the young person more real, someone who lives in the now, and the connection with eternity becomes all the more compelling: the hand cups three symbolic objects – an owl, arrow and acorn – whose symbolic function you recognize because Eisenman has made them all the same size, when in reality they are not. The figure lifts these three objects out of their normal world and presents them to us as symbols of wisdom, strength and motion (or progress). This gesture is further strengthened by borrowing a classic technique from art history: the figure is frozen in a moment, almost caught unaware, like in Rembrandt's portrait of Jan Six or the Syndics of the Drapers' Guild. This effect makes us wonder whether the symbols are being picked up or put down, whether they are being delivered to the courthouse or being taken out into the world. Through this rich fluidity, Eisenman beautifully shows us what a court of law can be: a place of exchange, connection and hopefully even consolation, just as in the works of Jesse Wine and Femmy Otten. Hopefully these help visitors to see, again and again, that they are not alone, that they are and always will be part of a greater whole – each with their own roles and responsibilities, though working together forever, connected.

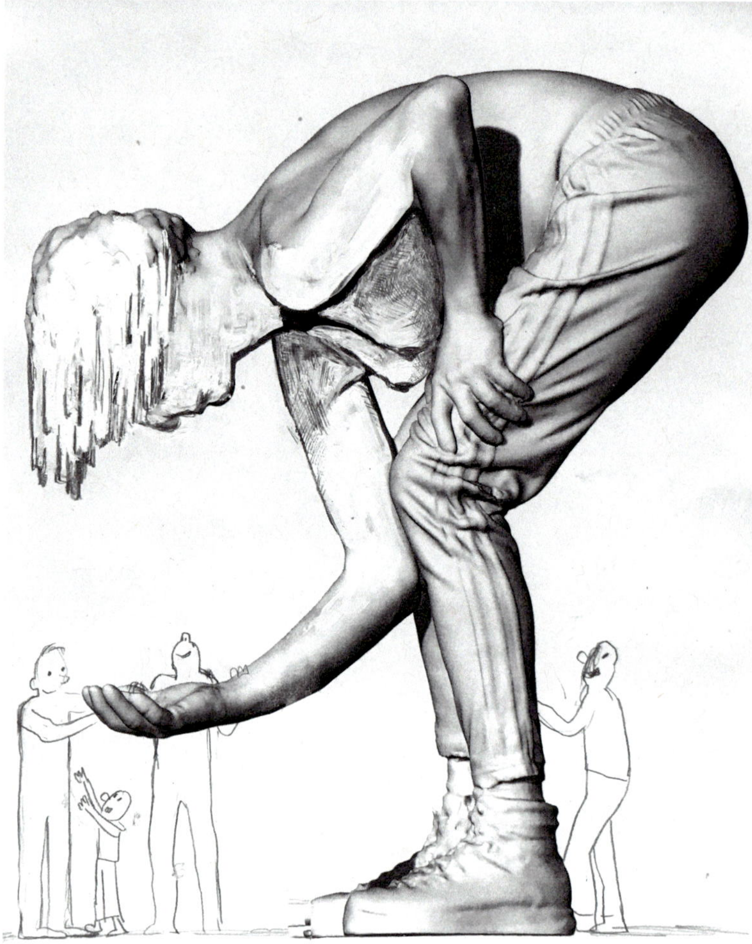

NICOLE EISENMAN, PROCESS IMAGES FOR *LOVE OR GENEROSITY*,
PHOTOS COURTESY OF THE ARTIST

II.

Occasionally in the middle of a trial, Judge Tjepco van Voorst Vader will let his eyes wander to a work of art. This is a very conscious decision. It is often when Van Voorst Vader has asked the two parties to come up with a solution to their impasse themselves, to propose the next step. The last thing he wants to do as a judge at this moment is to look either party directly in the eyes. That would communicate expectations and create inequality. At the same time, he cannot simply stare out into nothing, and so he looks at the art.

Everyone understands this gaze. Looking at art is the most familiar and legitimate way of briefly stepping outside of your world, your everyday environment. Just to be gone for a moment, escaping into other pictures, ideas or feelings, inspired by art that seems, initially anyway, to be far away from the present events. Of course, you can immediately be pulled back in when required.

From this perspective, the art spread throughout the new courthouse is very important. The building has an impressive presence, modernity and dignity, and it strikes precisely the right balance between expressing authority and humanity, which parallels what the law also seeks to do. The building itself is also its own world, and for this reason it was decided early on to fully integrate art into the spaces, which ultimately led to the installation of the works by Jesse Wine and Femmy Otten, and the figure – already hugely popular – on the square, *Love or Generosity* by Nicole Eisenman.

NICOLE EISENMAN,
LOVE OR GENEROSITY

Soon the realization dawned, however, that the Amsterdam Courthouse also has its own intriguing art collection, assembled by an internal art committee that has always tried to underscore the delicate balance between the law and the world. The budget was always limited, and yet, over the years the committee successfully accumulated a fine collection, consisting primarily of Dutch artists such as Ad Gerritsen, Koen Vermeulen, Janine van Oene, Kars Persoon, Toon Verhoef, Hans van den Ban, Marian Breedveld and Marjolein Rothman. Preliminary ideas centred on hanging the works in the 'Guggenheim' of the building: the breathtaking, round and open stairwell in the middle of the office floors. This space is reminiscent of the Guggenheim Museum in New York as well as M.C. Escher's criss-crossed stairs – so a perfect place for art. Once it became evident how well the works functioned in this space, the Courthouse quickly decided to hang up works from their collection in the public areas of the building.

And this works, too. On the superb marble walls of the courthouse, the works of art function as windows, vistas into the real world – though a softer, gentler version. This is mainly the result of the art committee's strategy of purchasing art that, first and foremost, could build a bridge between different worlds. Art that could provide some solace or a momentary departure, as much for visitors who have never been to court before and suddenly find themselves involved in an emotionally strenuous case, as for the staff who may benefit from withdrawing briefly from the dynamics of a case to collect their thoughts. Naturally, sustaining a goal of connection also imposes some limitations: the art in the courthouse must always seek to unite, never separate. This means that with every purchase, the art committee considers whether the art might unnecessarily provoke or offend anyone.

INEZ DE BRAUW 2500x1870 · MICHIEL HOOGEBOOM 2800x2000 · KOEN VERMEULE 3500x2000 · RINKE NIJBURG 3000x2000 · LIESBETH KRAAIJPOEL 1500x1500 · TON VAN DER WERF 1600x1000 · HAN SCHUIL 1600x1600 · M BREEDVELD 1500x2600 (2x) · KARS PERSOON 900x2200 · KARS PERSOON 500x2200

JANINE VAN OENE 3200x1780 · HENDRIK FLORE 1500x1200 1600x1200 · CLAUDY JONGSTRA 6700x2010 · GER LATASTER 790x570 (3x) · MARTIN HOFLAND 1400x900 · PAUL BEUMER 1910x1610 · AD GERRITSEN 1100x1250 · JEROEN VAN DE LAAR 1180x1180 · KOEN EBELING KONING 1100x1700

TOON VERHOEF 4850x4920 · H VAN DER PUTTEN 2400x2400 · E MATTHIJSSEN 2560x1960 · DANIEL VERKERK 820x740 · CORNEILLE 360x450 (7x) · BENOIT INNIS 500x600 (6x) · MAARTEN VERHAAK 510x370 (3x) · LUCASSEN 300x400 (3x) · O BOERWINKEL 900x800

SERGE GAME 1260x1090 · KEES KORTLANG 1400x1200 · MARLEEN VAN DIJK 600x800 · HJ WOLTER 800x580 · JOOP PLASMEIJER 500x400 · WILLEM WITSEN 600x530 · J BEUYS 300x210 (3x) · MATHIJSSEN 810x1110 · ED LEEFLANG, VINCENT VAN OJEN 370x250 (2x) · GINEKE SIKKEN 900x900 · SAM DRUKKER 650x650 · BAS MEERMAN 900x850

M ROTHMAN 800x1800 · KLAAS GUBBELS 950x900 · AD GERRITSEN 500x500 · BRAM VAN VELDE 640x460 · EMO VERKERK 650x500 · KOEN VERMEULE 810x470 · A FREIJMUTH 650x500 · FREDERIK ROES 320x400 (3x) · KARS PERSOON 110x130 (4x) · AD GERRITSEN 200x250

ROGER RAVEEL 770x570 · PETER ALMA 400x280 (8x) · VINCENT MENTZEL 300x450 · CARLA RODENBERG 580x480 · ED VAN DER ELSKEN 200x200 (8x) · ALOY OOSTERWIJK 220x340 (2x)

PETRA MOL 9000x3000x3000 · H. VAN DEN BAN 3200x1000x800 · HENK VISCH 2000x120x1650 · CH 1800x1580x260 · WIEN COBBENHAGEN 400x400x800 · HENNIE HOUTKOOP 320x120x90 290x140x140 · GERARDA DEMARTEAU 1420x270x270 · I DEKKER 520x320x80 · SCHAPEN DIMENSIONS UNKOWN

CHRIS DE BUEGER 400x180x180 · JEROEN HENNEMAN 800x150 · KLAAS GUBBELS 250x300x50 · CHANTAL VAN HEESWIJK 400x180x180 · FIOEN BLAISSE 1350x580x250 · LIA VAN VUGT 430x1090x1620 · MARIJKE SCHEFFERS 370x450x390

JEROEN VAN DE LAAR,
ALUMINIUM WANDRELIËF

INDRE URBONAITE,
STATE OF SHAME

CH, *UNTITLED*

H VAN DEN BAN, *UNTITLED*

So no nudes, no aggression, but also preferably no visible soles of the feet. When Femmy Otten was working on including a horse in one of her commissioned pieces and clearly making it a stallion, the discussions steered it towards the representation of a mare instead.

Beyond these limitations, there is more than enough left over in the world. Certainly, it is a world that focuses on the Netherlands: the art committee has purchased work almost exclusively from Dutch artists. They rarely look at the status or reputation of the artist. They visit art fairs, galleries and art events and they buy a bit impulsively, as long as there is a budget available and the committee feels that the work fits in with the atmosphere and intentions of a court of law. It is striking, for example, that there is little realism in the collection, in the sense of art that tries to copy reality. Representations of absurdity, alienation and surrealism are also practically absent. The art seems primarily to pursue the notion that reality is never one-dimensional, there is always more than one interpretation or truth, and it stimulates the visitor to look at reality more closely and intensely – which also means each individual is free to find their own way. And above all, that one's own vision really contributes something. Take the beautiful wall of portraits by painter Ad Gerritsen, who focuses on the individuality of his sitters with restrained brushstrokes and clear colours, exactly the approach as it should be in every courtroom. Or the powerful colour fields by Marian Breedveld, which afford you a moment of focus within the chaos of everyday life, or the snowy landscape by Serge Game that is so open it almost seems to breathe.

Perhaps one of the most beautiful and appropriate works in the Amsterdam Courthouse collection is *Certain Days, Certain Hours* by Erik Mattijssen. This work on paper shows what seems to be no more than a simple bedroom, presumably in a farmhouse given the wooden ceiling beams hung with baskets, the striped multicoloured carpet on the floor, and the twig in the flowerpot on the table against the blue sky of the open window. Mattijssen succeeds in drawing your attention to the extraordinary within the ordinary: you see – no, you know – this is a perfectly ordinary room, and yet by means of the artist's powerful and surprising perspective you are convinced that you are looking at a unique and matchless moment, and that there are so many of these. It is precisely this uniqueness, the respect for each moment and each person, that suits a courthouse so well: the understanding that everyone deserves to be seen and shown respect, whatever the circumstances. Justice is not only a system. It is a fair and compassionate mirror to the world. And the art here helps everyone in the courthouse, whether they are judges or visitors, to appreciate this.

INNSIDE
CMS

KAAN ARCHITECTEN

KAAN Architecten is a Dutch architecture firm with more than 30 years of experience in context-specific, timeless designs spanning a broad range of scales and typologies. Founded and led by Kees Kaan, Vincent Panhuysen and Dikkie Scipio from the headquarters in the heart of Rotterdam, the firm has expanded its international presence with satellite offices in São Paulo (2015) and Paris (2019), directed by Renata Gilio and Marylène Gallon respectively. Through a collaborative and analytical design approach, KAAN Architecten promotes Dutch building traditions of sustainability, welfare, pragmatism and quality. By merging practical and academic expertise, the firm responds to increasingly challenging complexities and contradictions in the built environment. Its body of work consists of civic, renovation and infrastructure projects as well as cultural, educational and urban developments for private or public clients. Widely acclaimed, the firm has been honoured with numerous international awards for architectural excellence.

RUUD BROUWERS

Ruud Brouwers is an architecture critic and writer. He was editor-in-chief of the journal *wonen-TA/BK* in the early 1970s and in this role influenced urban regeneration practices at the time. He advocated for more inspiring architecture, giving local residents a say, and revaluing the traditional city. He is one of the founders of the Netherlands Architecture Institute (NAi) and initiated the yearbook Architecture in the Netherlands. He chaired the committees for design approval and historic conservation in both Rotterdam and Maastricht and directed the Stimuleringsfonds voor Architectuur, a fund for stimulating quality in architecture.

HANS DEN HARTOG JAGER

Hans den Hartog Jager is a writer and art critic, based in Amsterdam. He writes reviews and has his own monthly column in the newspaper *NRC Handelsblad.* He has curated shows in different Dutch museums, the latest being *Brave New World, 16 Painters for the 21st Century*, in Museum De Fundatie, Zwolle. He is also the artistic director of Paradys, an international outdoor art project in Friesland, the Netherlands. Den Hartog Jager wrote more then ten books on art, including *Verf* (Paint, 2003), which contains interviews with the most prominent Dutch painters about their working methods, *Haai op sterk water* (Shark on formaldehyde, 2006), a collection of essays, *Het sublieme* (The sublime, 2011), an essay about the notion of beauty in contemporary art, *Het streven* (The Pursuit, 2014) about art and its influence in society.

KEES KAAN

From 1988 until 2013, Kees Kaan was the founding partner of Claus en Kaan Architecten. Kaan graduated from the Faculty of Architecture at Delft University of Technology in 1987. Since 2006 he has been professor of Architectural Design in Delft and initiator of the Complex Projects Chair, launched in 2012. The chair's research focuses on large-scale projects that characterize this era of rapid global urbanization. In 2019 Kaan was appointed chairman of the Architecture Department. In addition, he has been Principal Investigator at the Amsterdam Institute for Advanced Metropolitan Solutions (AMS) since 2016. Kaan is a lecturer and member of various juries and boards, both in the Netherlands and abroad.

VINCENT PANHUYSEN

Vincent Panhuysen joined Claus en Kaan Architecten in 1997 and became partner in 2002. Panhuysen began his training at the Amsterdam Technical School for Wood and Furniture Crafts, continuing his studies at the School of the Arts in Utrecht and the Rotterdam Academy of Architecture. This unique education allows him to exercise control over the entire building process, from concept to detailing. He is a frequent international lecturer with a focus on themes of contextuality and dialogue with the surroundings. For his special and careful guidance in the renovation of the Provinciehuis of North-Brabant, Panhuysen was awarded the 'Commissarispenning', a medal of merit from the King's Commissioner, Wim van de Donk, in 2015.

PROJECT CREDITS

Location
Parnassusweg 280, Amsterdam, the Netherlands
Client
Rijksvastgoedbedrijf (Central Government Real Estate Agency)
Program
public square, foyer, 50 courtrooms, offices, lobby, restaurant, conference center and library

Tender phase
October 2014 – February 2016
Design phase
May 2016 – December 2020
Construction phase
August 2017 – December 2020

GFA
60,200 m^2
Capacity
approximately 1,000 courthouse employees + 200 chain partners employees

Main contractor
Consortium NACH
Consortium NACH
Macquarie Capital: financer
ABT: technical advisor
DVP: management
KAAN Architecten: architect and interior architect
Heijmans: integral contractor
Facilicom: maintenance and facilities

KAAN Architecten Team
Michael Baas, Beatrice Bagnara, Sjoerd Boomars, Koen Bosman, Dennis Bruijn, Sebastiaan Buitenhuis, Robin Cals, Jana Culek, Sebastian van Damme, Marten Dashorst, Luuk Dietz, Cecilia Dobos, Ana Rivero Esteban, Paolo Faleschini, Raluca Firicel, Michael Geensen, Lisa Goes, Narine Gyulkhasyan, Thomas Hayat, Martine Huijsmans, Marlon Jonkers, Kees Kaan, Lianne Klitsie, Jasmijn Kok, Moritz Kuhl, Marco Lanna, Antony Laurijsen, Yinghao Lin, Johandry Martina, Marija Mateljan, Martina Margini, Julian O'Neale, Laura Ospina, Vincent Panhuysen, Kevin Park, Dikkie Scipio, Claudio Zampaglione
External team
Teun van Dooren (ABT), Siebe Besseling (ABT), Martijn Schuil (EGM)

CONSULTANTS
Structural engineering, geotechnics, building physics, MEP engineering, fire safety, acoustics, security
ABT, Velp
Parking
Wim van Vlierden, Rotterdam
Landscape architect
Simona Serafino Landscape Architect, Amsterdam
Roof design and safety
Kiwa BDA, Rijswijk
Metal stud wall consultant
Saint-Gobain Gyproc, Vianen

SUBCONTRACTORS & SUPPLIERS
MEP
Heijmans, Rosmalen
Fire safety and security
Trigion, Schiedam
Steel construction and facade cladding:
CSM Steel structures, Hamont-Achel (B)
Facade
TGM, Asten
Natural stone
Kolen Natuursteen, Eindhoven
Interior doors and windows
Smits, Gemert
Interior doors
Staalkozijn, Winterswijk
Metal stud walls
Muller afbouwgroep, Eindhoven
Ceilings and acoustics
Verwol Interior Systems, Delft/Opmeer
Climatized ceilings
Inteco, Boxtel
Partition wall systems
Maars Living Walls, Harderwijk
General fixed furniture maker
Smeulders Interieurgroep, Nuenen
Leather wall finishing (courtrooms)
Alphenberg Leather, Waalwijk
Lifts and escalators
Otis, Utrecht
Concrete work floors - upper floors
Red Betonbouw, Oud-Beijerland
Prefabricated concrete
Hoco Beton, Weert
Prefabricated concrete holding cells
Haitsma Beton, Kootstertille
Signage
De Vries Projekt Design, Eindhoven

ARTISTS
Public square work of art
Nicole Eisenman
Courtroom works of art
Femmy Otten
Courtyard works of art
Jesse Wine

COLOPHON

Concept
Marco Lanna, Vincent Panhuysen

Texts

Preface, Chapter introductions, Generously Functional
Ruud Brouwers

DBFMO: Good Architecture Is Paramount
Kees Kaan and Vincent Panhuysen

Participating in Architectural Design
Marco Lanna (interviewer)

Seemingly Effortless
Marten Dashorst

Art Makes Connections
Hans den Hartog Jager

Translation
Dianna Beaufort

Copy Editing
Dianna Beaufort, D'Laine Camp

Proofreading
D'Laine Camp

Design
Alice Colombo, Isabella Fiorante

Printing and Lithography
robstolk®, Amsterdam

Binding
Boekbinderij Patist, Zaltbommel

Paper
Circle print 95CIE, 115 gsm (interior)
Rebello 110, 350 gsm (cover material)

Photography

Sebastian van Damme: front and back cover images; 13; 63; 83, left; 84, top; 91; 92; 98, bottom left and bottom right; 116; 118, bottom; 119; 121, right
Fernando Guerra: 3; 10-11; 21; 22-23; 24; 25; 28-29; 36-37; 38; 39; 40; 41; 42-43; 44; 46; 47; 48-49; 57; 60; 81; 94; 95; 97; 124-125
Tom Philip Janssen: 108; 111; 112; 115; 118, top; 121, left
Marco Lanna: 100; 103
Dominique Panhuysen: 51; 67; 77; 83, right; 93; 98, left top and middle, right top and middle; 105
Vincent Panhuysen: 84, bottom

Thanks to Louise Attema, Fokke Van Dijk, Hans Janssen, Ton Schaap, Erik Tuijp

Publisher
Marcel Witvoet, nai010 publishers

Original drawings have been edited for security concerns.

Distribution and sales
nai010 publishers is an internationally orientated publisher specialized in developing, producing and distributing books in the fields of architecture, urbanism, art and design. www.nai010.com

nai010 books are available internationally at selected bookstores and from the following distribution partners:

North, Central and South America - Artbook | D.A.P., New York, USA, dap@dapinc.com

Rest of the world - Idea Books, Amsterdam, the Netherlands, idea@ideabooks.nl

For general questions, please contact nai010 publishers directly at sales@nai010.com or visit our website www.nai010.com for further information.

Printed and bound in the Netherlands

ISBN 978-94-6208-705-7
NUR 648
BISAC ARC000000
THEMA AM